Peter Dobereiner

GOLF RULES EXPLAINED

The ninth edition of the standard
work on the rules of golf,
fully revised and updated

W9-BBT-379

DAVID & CHARLES

For John and Robert, who saw what golf did for
their father and took to other games

A DAVID & CHARLES BOOK

First published in the UK as *Stroke, Hole or Match?* 1976
Republished as *Golf Rules Explained* in a revised edition 1980
Eighth edition 1992
Reprinted 1992, 1993, 1995
Ninth edition (revised) 1996

The pronouns 'he', 'him' and 'his' have been used for simplicity
throughout this work. Except in matters relating to Handicap and
Scratch Score, these pronouns should be taken to refer equally to
men and women

ISBN 0-7153-0494-1

Typeset by ABM Typographics, Hull
and printed in Great Britain by Butler & Tanner Ltd, Frome
for David & Charles
Brunel House   Newton Abbot   Devon

Contents

Introduction

Hardly a week passes without a new book on golf coming off the presses somewhere in the world. Millions of words about the game pour forth in different languages. They tell us how to play the game, about the history of golf and describe the personalities of the great players. The author of yet another golf book, therefore, bears a heavy responsibility for adding to the verbal cataract. So allow me to mount the penitent's stool and make a personal plea in justification of this book.

To be frank, I did not want to write it; I would much prefer that someone else had written it thirty years ago. That would have saved me much grief and anguish. But nobody did write it and so when I began to play golf I had only the haziest idea of the rudiments of the rules of golf. Some lucky beginners are weaned on golf, growing up under the guidance of fathers and friends wise in the ways of this absorbing game.

My apprenticeship was totally erratic. Like many golfers I picked up my knowledge of the rules in haphazard fashion like a bird scavenging for crumbs. Scraps of information – and misinformation – came my way and embarrassing experiences filled in some of the gaps. I still blush at the memory of holing a long putt only to have my elation turn sour at the caustic response of my opponent that I had lost the hole for striking the flagstick. Losing the hole was bad enough but being exposed as a golfing ignoramus was even worse.

The painful episode haunted me for weeks. It seemed so unfair. After all, there was no logic in it. What difference did it make if you putted with the flagstick in the hole? You could never make a shrewd guess, based on natural sporting instincts and common sense, that it would be wrong to hit the flagstick. I thought it all very unfair (and, as a matter of fact, I am still far from happy about that particular rule of which the only purpose it seems to me is to make the game slower).

Anyway, while my enthusiasm for golf grew, my respect for the rules remained dormant, to say the least. In due course I became professionally involved in golf as an author and journalist and had to absorb the rules as thoroughly as I could.

My hang-up about the wisdom of rules, or some of them, persisted and I delighted in writing articles in newspapers and magazines railing against the complexities and apparent anomalies of golf law. Basically, I reasoned, golf is a simple game – in the procedure, you understand, not the execution, which has always eluded me – and it requires only a few simple rules. The earliest surviving code, the articles of the Honourable Company of Edinburgh Golfers, 1744, had only thirteen rules and the last of these was really a special local rule: *Neither Trench, Ditch, nor Dyke made for the preservation of the Links, nor the Scholars' holes, nor the Soldiers' lines, shall be accounted a Hazard, but the Ball is to be taken out and Teed, and played with any iron Club.*

If our forefathers could get along happily enough on the iron rations of a dozen basic rules, why do we need sixteen paragraphs on etiquette, forty-one definitions, thirty-four rules with clauses, sub-clauses and appendices as numerous as the grains of sand in Hell bunker? And that is just the basic skeleton of golf law. In addition it is fleshed out with fat volumes of case law in the form of Decisions which have been handed down by the Rules of Golf Committee on appeal.

The moment of my deepest disenchantment with this unwieldy structure of legalistic rigmarole came during the Ryder Cup match at St Louis in 1971 between the United States and Great Britain and Ireland. In the four-ball series of the second day, Arnold Palmer and Gardner Dickinson were playing against Bernard Gallacher and Peter Oosterhuis. The Americans had the honour on the par-3 7th hole. The caddies for the match were college students who were naturally enough delighted at the opportunity to spend a week in the company of their heroes.

For them it was the chance of a lifetime. No one except a churl could blame Gallacher's student caddie for excitedly asking Palmer what club he had used for his towering shot to the green 208 yards distant. 'Heck! It looked to be only a mid-iron.' Palmer replied, 'Five-iron.' Gallacher did not hear this whispered exchange at the side of the tee because by now he was addressing his ball. But the referee heard it and instantly recognised a breach of the rule which forbids the asking of advice from anyone except your own partner of either of your own caddies. The referee conferred with two distinguished and learned committeemen and after the hole had been completed as a half in 3s, the referee gave his decision: the British pair had lost the hole. Naturally the incident caused considerable embarrassment all round, not least to Palmer himself, and there was much comment from members of both teams along the lines that such a purely technical infringement would have been better dismissed by an attack of diplomatic deafness on the part of the referee.

I felt no outrage at the decision but was appalled at the treasure hunt through the rule book which was needed to track down the decision. A whole series of points had to be established. Was Gallacher responsible for the action of his caddie? Did the caddie's question: 'Great shot! What club did you hit?' constitute the seeking of advice under the meaning of the definition? If so, it being a four-ball, was Gallacher only to be penalised or did any penalty apply to Oosterhuis as well? And finally, what was the appropriate penalty – loss of hole or disqualification? Hours later, after much private conferring in committee with deep research into the law books, an official statement was issued tracing the legal process through two definitions and three rules of golf. As a matter of incidental interest I had done a personal search through the rules and after a number of restarts from false clues I had arrived at the conclusion that the British pair should not have lost the hole. The correct ruling, by my researches, was disqualification. That experience brought home to me more strongly than ever a guilty realisation of my ignorance of the rules. And that was just silly. Here I was, paid to write about golf and interpret it for my readers and I could not honestly say that I knew the rules of the game. Actually that was not quite as absurd as it may sound because very few people are fully conversant with every ramification of every rule. Every year we find examples of men who have played golf professionally all their lives who accidentally infringe a rule through ignorance.

Anyway, from the time of that Ryder Cup ruling I decided that since I could not influence the lawmakers to simplify the rules, I would just have to buckle down and make a thorough study of those 41 definitions and 34 rules and all those confusing sub-clauses. My first conclusion came as a great surprise. After years of complaining about the excess of verbosity in the rules, I discovered that they were written with the greatest economy. How often I had scoffed at the superfluity of paragraph 7 in the preamble to the United States Golf Association's version of the rules: *Every word means what it says.* In fact, that is an important point to bear in mind when reading the rules, which are absolutely precise. And while they may have about them the arid and stilted style of all legal literature, they also possess a certain elegance. The trouble about them, of course, is that being set out in legal style, using words such as 'hazard' where we golfers commonly talk of 'bunker' of 'trap', the lay mind finds them difficult to absorb.

For most of us, accustomed to reading books and newspapers and absorbing the general sense of what is written without paying close attention to precise detail, there is not much difference, for example, between the expression 'a club' and 'the club'. To the golf lawyer there is a vital distinction and that tiny difference can involve a penalty. Rule 14, for example, says that the ball *must be fairly struck at with the head of the club and must not be pushed, scraped or spooned.* There was an appeal to the Rules of Golf Committee from a player whose ball had lodged firmly in a pine tree. The tree was so thick that the player felt it was useless to try to dislodge it with one club. He therefore grasped a bundle of three clubs and smashed into the tree with this battery of ironmongery. The ball popped out on to the green but the player was penalised for using three clubs. He appealed against the ruling on the grounds that he did not honestly believe he had made contact with the ball with one club, let alone three of them. The Committee upheld the penalty decision because of that word 'the'. 'The club' can only mean one club and so Rule 14 had been infringed.

The one rule which survives in the essential sense from that earliest Edinburgh code reads: *He whose Ball lyes farthest from the Hole is obliged to play first.* I once felt that the lawmakers should have retained that wording if only as a reminder of golf's ancient origins. After all, it says everything a golfer needs to know. But does it? The modern rule (10) reads: *When the balls are in play, the ball farther from the hole shall be played first. If the balls are equidistant from the hole, the option of playing first shall be decided by lot.* Grudgingly I have to admit that the modern version is more precise, even if only because it gives tacit recognition to women golfers by eliminating 'He' and by making provision for the equidistant situation.

Comprehensive and unambiguous as the Rules may be, the ordinary golfer may be forgiven if he is reminded of George Bernard Shaw's dictum that all the learned professions are conspiracies against the public. He was referring, of course, to the private languages which doctors and accountants and, above all, lawyers invent so that we uninitiated laymen must pay them fat fees to unravel our problems. Lawyers are always strongly represented on the Rules of Golf committees and it shows in the archaic language which makes the rules so difficult to assimilate and remember. Who in everyday life would use the expression 'ball in motion'? We would say 'moving ball'. When did you last use the word 'deem' in conversation with your friends or family? Shakespeare's Dick the Butcher was being rather too radical for golfing purposes when he proposed: 'The first thing we do, let's kill all the lawyers.' But a certain constraint on our learned friends' influence would do wonders for the Rules of Golf. By all means let the lawyers ensure in committee that all contingencies are fully and precisely covered but then let someone with expert command of the English language render the rule in plain, everyday prose.

It was the problem of legalistic interpretation which convinced me that a book would be useful if it could present the rules in simple, everyday terms in such a way as to make them understandable and memorable. In no sense is this book intended to be a substitute for the official version. My aim has been to provide an introduction to the main rules (I have omitted some of the more esoteric ones such as the technical specifications for clubs and balls) so that the beginner will have a grounding in the laws and will be able to refer to the official rules when necessary with the confidence of knowledge. At the same time I have tried to distil and explain the philosophy behind the rules since it is always easier to act correctly if you understand and respect the reason for the things you are required to do. I hope that such explanations will reduce some of the undoubted sources of confusion. For instance, there is a rule (8) which includes the provision that you must not have a mark placed on the line of your shot (such as parking a caddie car on the skyline for a blind shot) or have anyone stand close to the line while you play the stroke.

In a tournament in England a player called a penalty on another competitor because the caddie held up the flagstick to indicate the line of a blind shot to the hole. In fact, there should have been no penalty because another rule (17) specifically permits the flagstick to be held up to indicate the position of the hole, regardless of where the player may be. That incident, which unhappily resulted in a player being wrongfully disqualified, also illustrates another side of the rules. Most people see rules – and indeed laws of all kinds – as a series of prohibitions carrying penalties for the transgressor. Woe betide us if we break the law. But the rules should not be seen solely as a list of 'Thou shalt not' commandments. They also incorporate the golfer's Bill of Rights and that is another good reason for knowing them thoroughly. The case histories of golf are full of tragic examples of players who have lost important competitions simply because they were not sure of their rights. There is nothing unsporting about using the rules to your advantage wherever possible. Indeed, it can happen that if you sportingly decline an opportunity to take your due advantage, then you actually become liable to a penalty. A famous example occurred at the British Open Championship at Troon in 1973. Tony Jacklin's ball landed in a rabbit hole and under the provision of Rule 25 he dropped the ball without penalty two club-lengths clear of the nearest point of relief. That was under the old rule. Relief is now one club-length. On hitting the ground the ball rolled a few feet further from the rabbit hole and into a much better lie. Jacklin did not know his rights in this case. (The rules permit a dropped ball to roll *a further* two club-lengths, making four club-lengths in all in those days, now three club-lengths, from its original position so long as it does not finish nearer the hole.) Jacklin felt that this lucky roll was giving him an undue advantage and in a spirit of fair play he picked up his ball to drop it again. His action was seen and he was duly penalised for touching his ball when it was in play. Quite possibly Jacklin's good intentions and instincts for fair play on that occasion cost him the championship.

The lesson must be to play to the letter of the law, accepting its bounties as well as its penalties, with equal grace. The laws, which are administered by the Rules of Golf Committees of the Royal and Ancient Golf Club of St Andrews and the United States Golf Association, and jointly revised every four years, try to be fair. But no rule can legislate for every case which may arise in a game played over such a diversity of country as a golf course. For every golfer there will be occasions when the application of a rule will appear totally unjust or absurdly benevolent.

Accept them both, according to the letter of the law. But there will also be times so unusual that no rule of golf covers the situation. Then you can safely give rein to your sense of fair play and natural justice. The rules say so. They call it equity. Use it sparingly even in social golf games with your friends. In the long run both you and your friends will get more satisfaction from your golf it you meticulously adhere to the rules. And by cultivating the habit of being a stickler for the rules you will greatly reduce the danger of embarrassment or disappointment when you come to play in serious competition.

Sometimes the official interpretation of an otherwise sensible Rule of Golf is so outlandish as to defy belief. The useful American word 'whammy' seems to fit these occasions. The victims of these digressions through the looking glass of golf law did not find them amusing when they were clobbered by the full weight of the law. But time lends a certain enchantment to the wilder aberrations of those who seek to keep us on the path of legal righteousness and so, in the interests of enlightenment and entertainment, I have included a number of whammies in the appropriate places.

In the chapters which follow I have noted the rule numbers in parenthesis during discussion of each point and suggest that you will benefit greatly from references to the official rules as you go along.

MAIN CHANGES OF RULE
Effective 1 January 1996

The four-yearly revisions to the Rules of Golf, effective from 1 January 1996, contain no rule changes of substance, merely minor adjustments to existing Rules and alterations in wording to clarify points of ambiguity.

In a move intended to strengthen the position of the authorities against slow play, the Rules of Golf committees have introduced a provision that tournament committees may establish pace of play guidelines and add a single stroke penalty as a first offence option for slow play in stroke-play. Subsequent penalties will continue to be a two-stroke penalty and ultimately disqualification. The apparent anomaly of clamping down on slow play by reducing the penalty is explained by the fact that the traditional two-stroke penalty was so severe that committees were reluctant, often to the point of dereliction of clear duty, to impose it. This was particularly the case in competitions promoted by the rule-making authorities who should have been setting an example to the sport. Professional bodies were so set against the two-stroke penalty that they adopted special tournament rules substituting a trifling monetary fine for the two-stroke penalty.

Another loudly trumpeted revision enables committees to adopt a local rule designed to protect environmentally sensitive areas on golf courses. The purpose for this revision seems to be largely a propaganda exercise to demonstrate golf's commitment to the politically fashionable subjects of the environment and golf courses as nature reserves. Certainly it is difficult to detect any legal imperative for making a special rule. For years golf courses have supported nature reserves and dedicated them as no-go areas for golfers by the simple expedient of marking them out-of-bounds. The preservation of rare botanical specimens at Royal St George's golf club, Sandwich, England, and a reserve for a colony of seed-eating birds within the boundary of Durban Country Club, South Africa, come to mind.

1 | ON THE TEE

KNOW YOUR OWN BALL (12)

Before starting a round of golf you have an important responsibility – to make sure that you can identify your ball. As we shall presently see, there are severe penalties for playing a wrong ball. Even the wide variety of manufacturers' markings are inadequate to guarantee that two players in a four-ball are not using balls of the same brand and number. Most professionals add a distinctive personal mark with the point of a pencil, such as dotting the 'o' of 'Dunlop', to eliminate any possibility of later confusion. There is no need for the ordinary club player to go to these lengths. All that is necessary is for you to tell the other players in your group the brand and number of your ball. Then any duplicate can be exchanged before you hit off. However, if you run low on ammunition and have to play a similar ball to one someone else of your group is using, give it a distinguishing mark. It is a rule of life rather than a golfing law but at the start of a match you should always inform your opponent of the brand and number of your ball.

On the subject of ball markings it might be worth mentioning a useful convention in the event of a lost ball. If you hit into heavy rough and opponents or fellow competitors join you to look for it, as hopefully they will, it is a good idea to repeat the brand and number as you begin the search. That policy eliminates any possibility of friction arising from someone finding a ball and asking 'What were you playing?'. It is a natural enough question to ask but it can be misinterpreted as a cross-examination to guarantee that you do not claim a ball that was not yours. As if you would! So start the hunt by shouting 'I'm playing a Maxfli 6' and then if any other ball is found it can safely be picked up by the finder without suspicion or embarrassment.

LEARN THE RULES (6)

A further important preliminary to a game of golf is to familiarise yourself with any local rules, which should be printed on the score card or posted on the club notice board. You will get no sympathy by complaining that you did not realise that a certain path was out of bounds. The rules emphasise the responsibility of the golfer to familiarise himself with the laws of the game and the special local rules and, as in the larger game of life, ignorance of the law is never acceptable as an excuse. In any case it is only sensible to read the local rules. It has happened to every golfer that during a round he gets into trouble, consults the back of the card and then moans: 'If I'd known it was out of bounds over here I'd never have played that shot.' Local rules, like the other rules, can help a player as well as hinder him. In this game we need all the help we can get, so take a minute or two to absorb the local rules.

FOURTEEN CLUBS (4)

Another duty before teeing off is to check that you do not have more than fourteen clubs with you. That is the legal limit and this is an appropriate point to introduce one of the basic philosophies on which the whole structure of golfing law is based. Despite what the frustrated golfer might imagine as he grapples with the complexities of the official code of rules, with its myriad clauses and sub-clauses, the rules basically derive from common sense. When a golfer is unsure of a rule, he should ask himself the question: 'What is the fair and logical thing for me to do in this situation?' On most occasions the answer suggested by common sense will be correct under the laws. Take this fourteen club rule. You are out playing and you accidentally break a club. Can you replace it? Yes, you can, common sense tells you, because you will still be within the fourteen club limit. And that it what the rule says. (Mind you, that does not mean you can run back to the club from the far end of the course to fetch a replacement from your locker. Then you would be infringing the rule against playing without undue delay (6). But common sense tells you that, too.)

The same logic suggests that *deliberately* breaking a club, such as snapping your putter across your knee in a fit of pique, is a different kettle of fish entirely. That's nobody's fault but your own and, just as common sense makes it obvious that after such temper tantrums clubs cannot be replaced, so do the rules of golf.

There is one practical complication about the fourteen club rule. Manufacturers normally make clubs in sets of four woods, eight or nine irons, wedge, sand-wedge and putter. A so-called full set of sixteen is therefore illegal. In theory, the golfer who owns such a beautiful quiver of clubs is supposed to take notice of such factors as the weather and the state of the course, and then discard those clubs he thinks will be of least use to him. But all too often he omits that ritual and discovers on the first tee that there are 15 or 16 clubs in his bag. Must he now drag all the way back to the clubhouse or his car to discard the unwanted ones and keep his companions kicking their heels on the tee, possibly missing their place in the starting time? Yes. But a player who discovers an extra club during the round and takes his penalty can declare that club out of play.

Penalties for carrying excess clubs, *regardless of the number of extra clubs in the bag,* are as follows:

Match-play: loss of each hole on which the violation occurred with a maximum penalty per round of loss of two holes.
Stroke-play: two penalty strokes on each hole on which the violation occurred, with a maximum penalty of four strokes.
Stableford: deduct two points from the final tally for each hole on which a violation occurred, with a maximum penalty deduction of four points.

14 CLUB WHAMMY

In view of the stringent rules on the number of clubs and the circumstances in which they can be replaced, it may seem odd that in one instance the player has complete licence to do what suits him best. A recent Decision makes it clear that in measuring off distances, as in two club-lengths from an unplayable lie, the player can use 'any club'. Does that mean he can borrow one of those dreadful broom-handle putters from a fellow competitor? Yes, he can. Can he borrow one from a different group? Yes, from anyone within range provided he does not unduly delay play. But would not such a procedure temporarily bring the player's complement of clubs up to 15, thus exceeding the legal limit, and would it not constitute a sneaky infringement of the spirit of the game? Yes indeed, but it is entirely lawful. Whammy.

THE TEEING GROUND

With those preliminaries out of the way, we are now ready to go on to the tee, which is the area of prepared ground at the beginning of each hole. We are concerned with that part of the tee called the teeing ground, a rectangle extending back two club-lengths from a line between the markers. (The rules of golf make frequent mention of this measurement of 'two club-lengths'. By all means measure off with the longest club in your bag and take fullest advantage of this wording when it suits your purpose.) The ball must be teed-up within the rectangle although you may stand outside it if you wish (11). For instance, if the area is particularly worn you may well want to tee the ball at the extreme backward limit of the teeing ground and in that case your right foot would be outside the teeing ground. But beware of teeing-up too far forward. We all need every inch of advantage, or think we do, and it is very easy on occasion to tee-up in front of the markers, especially if they are not set exactly square to the line of shot. Now we may be in trouble unless some kindly soul points out the error before the ball is hit.

In stroke play if you hit from outside the teeing ground, you are penalised two strokes and must then play from within the teeing ground. Any strokes played from outside the teeing ground do not count. If you fail to rectify your mistake before you tee off on the next hole (or leave the 18th green) you are disqualified – you will not have completed the stipulated round (1).

In match-play your opponent can recall a shot played from outside the teeing ground and make you play again. In that case there is no penalty. The humiliation is punishment enough without making you count that first, foul shot.

BALL FALLING OFF TEE-PEG (11)

Having teed up your ball in the right place, it commonly happens that the ball falls off the tee-peg or is knocked off it by the club-head at address. Well, the answer to that one is usually that some comedian calls out: 'One!' The Rules of Golf Committee has so far failed to devise a suitable penalty for those guilty of perpetrating the oldest joke in golf, so that player's only redress in the matter is to shrivel the wretch with a telling response. As for the ball, it can be replaced on its tee with no penalty.

However, if you have actually started your downswing

when the ball topples from its tee, that is just too bad unless you can check the downswing before the club-head reaches the ball. If you can check the downswing then no damage is done because that does not constitute a stroke. Let us assume that you are unable to check your downswing and the ball toppling from its tee is missed entirely or caught a glancing blow. You have to count that stroke and, since the ball is now in play, you cannot replace the ball on its tee peg.

THE HONOUR (10)

With our clubs duly counted and the identity of the ball established, the round can begin. Who is going to hit first? This is called taking the honour and although it is seldom of any great practical consequence, it is a distinctive part of golfing ritual and an important reminder that golf is an honourable game based on sportsmanship. In organised competitions, the players hit off the 1st tee in the order in which they appear in the draw. If there is no official list, then the honour is decided by lot, in the legal terminology. In other words, you toss a coin for it. But most golf is played socially at club level and in this case there is a long established convention for the player with the lowest handicap to hit first. Equal handicaps toss for it.

A note of caution must be sounded at this point. That convention about the lower handicap man playing the first shot in friendly games is one of several customs which have grown up in golf but which are at variance with the rules. What difference does it make, you ask? None at all! It is only a harmless and generous gesture of respect towards the superior skill of the better players. If the law condemns it then the law is an ass! If we want to play it that way, who is to stop us? The answer is that nobody will stop you. The custodians of the laws of golf are not in the slightest degree interested in how golfers behave in their private games of purely social golf. But if you habitually give the low-handicap player the honour in private matches, it is quite possible that you will automatically follow the same practice in an official competition, such as a club medal tournament.

Now the whole legal apparatus of golfing officialdom does become involved because the first rule of the tournament will be (or certainly should be): *The competition will be conducted under the Rules of Golf as approved by the Royal and Ancient Golf Club of St Andrews and the United States Golf Association.* Any query will be referred to one of these two bodies for arbitration. And they, you may be sure, will have no truck with any excuses such as 'But we always do it like that at our club.' The law says the honour shall be decided by lot and that's that.

It is no use pointing out that there is no penalty for playing out of turn in stroke-play. That applies only in taking the honour by mistake. If you have tacitly conspired with your fellow competitor to ignore the rule and follow the usual convention, then you are automatically guilty of a breach of Rule 1 which forbids, under penalty of disqualification, any agreement to waive a rule. You could be ordered to give back a prize. The sensible thing, surely, is to bury the convention about low-handicap men hitting off first and get into the habit of tossing a coin. That settles the question of who hits first. From then on the honour goes to the player with the lowest score on the previous hole. If the hole is completed with the same scores, the honour does not change. In match-play, if you mistakenly steal the honour by playing out of turn off the tee, your opponent can demand that you abandon that ball and play another in your proper turn. There is no penalty other than the embarrassment, just as in the case of playing from outside the teeing ground.

There is no power of recall in stroke-play and no penalty. The ball is in play right enough but stealing the honour is an act of discourtesy and if committed deliberately for purposes of giving a player an advantage the committee of a competition will impose a penalty.

STROKE AND DISTANCE

There are not very many more ways you can fall foul of the law on the tee, and you may feel there are just about enough since you have not yet struck a ball, but the possibilities which remain are of the highest importance and should be thoroughly absorbed. They cover the procedure for lost ball, out of bounds or ball unplayable, and these rules, which apply right through the game, form the very foundation of golf law. We will examine them in detail later. For the present let us concentrate on one of golf's earliest precepts.

From the time men first began to play golf, whenever that was and wherever it may have been, they held to the principle that the ball must be played as it lies (13).

We can tell from the specialised clubs, such as rut irons and water-mashies, how reluctant our forefathers were to deviate from that cardinal brief. We must still honour that central concept of playing the ball as it lies. That ought to be an article of faith for every golfer even though the rules nowadays permit many deviations from the original ideal. But right from the start men ran into predicaments which made it impossible to continue the game without some form of escape clause. After all, if your ball was lost in a lake, you had to do something about it. So came into being the stroke-and-distance rule. Down the centuries golfers have scratched their heads and asked 'What do I do about that?' and their opponents have answered 'Stroke and distance.'

So let us get this stroke-and-distance rule firmly established because that is the principle from which many variations in golf law flow. If your ball is lost, or out of bounds, or is stuck up a tree or, as once happened, has fallen down the chimney of a greenkeeper's cottage and plopped into a pan of stew simmering on the hob, you can invoke the stroke-and-distance rule. You may go back to the place from which you hit the last shot (in this case you are still on the tee), play another ball and add one penalty stroke to your score. Stroke and distance is the blanket rule which covers all occasions – your next shot off the tee is your third. If you play another ball from the tee under the stroke-and-distance rule you are at liberty to tee-up the ball again.

RULE 1

As we replace the head covers on our drivers and walk up the fairway, let us reflect on some of the other basic precepts of this absorbing game of golf. Take Rule 1 which simply says: *The game of golf consists in playing a ball from the teeing ground into the hole by a stroke or successive strokes in accordance with the rules. Penalty for breach of rules: match-play – loss of hole; stroke-play – disqualification!* What does it mean? On the face of it the rule appears so obvious as to be unnecessary. Taking the component parts of the rule separately it can be made to sound so banal as to be absurd. *Playing a ball* – well, what else?...*from teeing ground into the hole* well, no one would try it the other way round...*in accordance with the rules* – so you have to obey the rules; there's a novelty! In fact, Rule 1 serves an important purpose because even some of those obvious provisions can be broken. Golfers have frequently missed their way on strange courses and holed out on, say, the seventh green thinking it to be the sixth. Rule 1 covers that situation.

In another case, on a course where two holes had teeing grounds of successive holes next to each other, some players hit tee shots from both tees to save themselves the labour of walking back the length of the first of the two holes. That practice was ruled contrary to Rule 1 because they did not complete the round in successive strokes. But Rule 1's most important purpose is to give competition committees blanket powers to deal with irregularities. Most rules carry their own individual scale of punishments which are laid down to cover accidental infringements. But serious or deliberate offences – let us not be mealy-mouthed about it, that means cheating – clearly need to be punished more severely, and in such cases Rule 1 can be invoked.

Perhaps a brief note on the morality of golf is in order at this point. It is very easy to cheat at golf. Probably no other game offers more scope to unscrupulous players who are willing to take advantage of the fact that they are often hundreds of yards away from any witness. The ball can often be nudged up on to a friendly tuffet during the address with no risk of detection. In the rough the lie can be improved in many clandestine ways. One of golf's jokes concerns a foursome match (in which partners take alternate shots at the same ball). One player hit into dreadful jungle and his partner disappeared into the undergrowth where he was heard thrashing about wildly. 'Is it playable?' shouted the first golfer and received the classic reply 'Not yet.' That story may or may not strike you as funny but in real life cheating is not amusing. It happens, of course, even at the highest level and scandals rock the game from time to time. But golf is a game of trust and the vast majority of players treat it as such.

That does not mean that golfers as a breed are necessarily more honest than other people. It simply reflects the fact that golf is a diversion. It is meant to give the player pleasure. And while golfers find different pleasures and satisfactions in the game according to their natures, there is precious little sense of accomplishment to be had from returning a good score or winning a match by cheating. In this respect golf is like patience. No one stops you cheating at patience but what fun is there in 'getting out' if you manipulate the cards to gain that end? The exercise loses its point and so it is with golf.

SUNNINGDALE RULE

Once you have mastered the Rules in all their rich diversity you may be tempted from time to time to flaunt your knowledge. In a single round of golf you might very well have the opportunity to take your fellow competitors to task half a dozen times for minor breaches of procedure. If you did this you would quickly acquire the reputation as an interfering busybody. Pretty soon your fellow members will be dodging behind pillars at your approach and if you do meet one face to face he may well rebuff your query about getting a game with the response: 'Sorry, old chap, but our threesome is already made up.' If you see a fellow competitor or an opponent about to follow a wrong procedure which will cost him a penalty stroke or two, then you are duty bound to warn him and put him on the right track. Be diplomatic about how you issue your warning. Adopt a spirit of helpfulness because a belligerent yell of 'Are you accusing me of trying to cheat?' will ruin everybody's day. The expert rulesman should also avoid parading his piety when he is taking relief under the Rules. Commonly he will put on a sanctimonious voice when he says: 'I say, old chap, would you mind taking a gander at my ball. I'm convinced it is in casual water but I'd appreciate your confirmation.' What he is really saying is: 'Observe the great rules expert making doubly sure that he does not gain an unfair advantage. Such meticulous behaviour represents sportsmanship at its best.' Sunningdale golf club, that bastion of golf's traditions, has an unofficial rule that if anyone asks (about taking free relief in particular) the answer has to be 'No'. That is not a bad rule for all of us to follow. If you are convinced that you are due relief from, say, ground under repair, go ahead and take it. If you think a second opinion is needed, then that slight doubt must dictate your actions: play the ball as it lies.

STROKE- AND MATCH-PLAY

Everyone who is interested in golf enough to have read this far will know that there are two forms of the game – stroke-play (counting the total number of shots for a round) and match-play (played by holes). The rules for these two forms of the game vary slightly, as we have already seen in the matter of playing out of turn on the tee. Various studies have been made from time to time with the object of simplifying the rules so that the same code and the same scale of penalties could apply for both stroke- and match-play. One anomaly in the dual system, for example, is that the general penalty in stroke-play is two shots (3) and loss of hole in match-play (2). Now for a first-class golfer who can be expected to play 18 holes in 72 shots the stroke-play penalty is 1/36th part of a round while the loss of hole penalty is double, 1/18th part. For humbler players the discrepancy is even more marked. All attempts at unifying the rules have so far foundered – on the rock of tradition rather than because of insuperable legal problems, many of us feel – so for the moment there is nothing else for it but to learn both sets of rules. As if the poor beginner did not have difficulty enough in mastering one lot! In practice there are not too many pitfalls in the dual code. The majority of the rules apply to both forms of golf and circumstances will normally dictate when and how the match-play variations should be applied.

The one danger to avoid is to try and play both forms simultaneously. If you are playing a match do not say to your opponent: 'If you don't mind I'll mark a card as well for handicapping purposes.' When you proudly report your victory to the competition secretary he is likely to award the match to your opponent – and reject your card for handicap adjustment as well. The reason for this ban on what might appear to be a harmless, indeed convenient, practice is that there are significant variations in the rules for the two forms of golf which make it impractical to play both forms simultaneously.

2 | THROUGH THE GREEN

Golf is a lonely game. In spite of its associations with conviviality and sociable club life, it is essentially a highly introverted pastime. At every level of the game the golfer is on his own the moment he steps up to address his ball. His friends are silent (or so we hope) and retreat from the golfer's consciousness. Now it is just him, a club and a ball. In theory there ought to be no great difficulty about hitting the ball. It requires no great physical strength to swing a club weighing less than a pound – although we may think it needs all the exertion we can produce. The action of swinging a club is not complicated or difficult – although most of us make it so. And the degree of precision needed to implant the club-face flush to the ball is no greater than a hundred everyday actions which we unerringly perform without conscious thought. If you swat a sitting fly and knock the head of a daisy with a walking stick, then you can play golf.

If we could play golf with the same conditioned instincts we would have no problem. But we cannot. The fact is that golf is difficult because we make it so. All manner of inhibitions and fears rise up in the mind of a man about to hit a golf ball, some of them demons of his own creation and some impressed on to his imagination by the daunting sight of the way ahead.

There is nothing like an expanse of water, for instance, to produce an involuntary tightening of the hands on the grip and a resolve to give this one a little bit of extra effort. And then, usually in combination with an irresistible urge to look up and see the result of the shot, the golfer is lost. What was basically a straightforward pitch shot has turned into a feverish ordeal entirely through the interaction of past memories, self-doubts and visual forebodings in the mind of the golfer.

So the golfer is really playing against himself. He is his own enemy far more than any flesh and blood opponent. Golf is therefore much more than a test of manual skill and dexterity. It is also a trial of character and the rules reflect this aspect of the game. We have already touched on one element of this side of golf in discussing the heavy degree of trust which golf lays on the honesty of the player.

ADVICE AND ASSISTANCE (8)

The loneliness of the golfer is further emphasised by the ban on receiving advice and assistance. The rule says you must ask or receive advice only from your partner or either of your caddies. Advice is defined as any suggestion which could influence you in making up your mind about how to play, what club to use or what type of shot to attempt. Information about rules or local rules is specifically exempted from the rule, so although the answer to a question such as 'Is it out of bounds over that fence?' might well influence you in planning your shot, it is allowable. But 'What club did you hit?' as we saw in the case of Bernard Gallacher in the 1971 Ryder Cup match, is construed as asking for advice. It has also been ruled that asking if the flagstick is on the back or front of the green does not constitute seeking advice since it is public information and simply saves the player walking forward to see for himself.

Similarly, you can ask anyone the line of play, such as 'Is this a dog-leg to the right?' Another seemingly mad part of the rule prohibits you from seeking physical assistance in making a stroke, such as having a friend steady your trembling hands on the putter and guiding the club for you, or from accepting protection from the elements. So do not allow your caddie to hold an umbrella over you when you are making a stroke.

It is in this area of pernickety regulations that the rules of golf could possibly be simplified. That ban on physical assistance, plus Rule 14 about forbidding the ball to be pushed, scraped or spooned and a few others are so outlandish and obvious that they could surely be incorporated into one blanket rule requiring that the game be played in accordance with established custom and tradition.

NO MARK ON LINE (8)

The final part of the advice-and-assistance rule is one of the least known (or least observed) laws of golf. It says that through the green you may have the line of play indicated to you by anyone but no one may stand on or near the line as you play your shot and any mark placed on the line must be removed before you make your stroke. This rule is frequently broken on undulating courses which involve blind shots. A player walks uphill to survey the way ahead, parks his bag or caddie car on the skyline and then returns to his ball, carrying the selected club. The shot is then played directly over the mark on the skyline, often in ignorance of the rule but illegally for all that. A two stroke penalty or loss of hole should be imposed.

This is the rule *through the green* and is superseded by the laws covering the green itself. You can have the flagstick held up to indicate the position of the hole at any time, whether you are on the green or not.

One innocent trap awaits the unwary in this prohibition about putting a mark on the line. In their instruction books, many great players such as Jack Nicklaus advocate selecting a mark, such as a daisy, just in front of the ball and then hitting over that mark. That is fine. But if there is no suitable mark on your intended line you might be tempted to pick a daisy and place it in front of the ball. And that would never do.

NO IMPROVING OF LIE OR LINE (13)

By now the precept of playing the ball as it lies will be well understood. That thought can be extended to the wider principle that the golfer must accept the consequence of his previous shot. If you are in trouble then you have to play out of that trouble as you find it. We will come to the exception to that precept – such as an unplayable lie, impediments and obstructions – in another chapter but for the moment we will stay with situations which, however unpleasant, are free of such complications. The rule says that you must not improve the lie of your ball or the line of the shot or the area of your swing *by moving, bending or breaking anything fixed or growing, or by removing or pressing down sand, loose soil, cut turf placed in position or other irregularities of surface which could in any way affect your lie.* Obviously, if your ball is in a thicket you could not get to it without bending anything growing so the rule provides specific exceptions. These are: *in fairly taking your stance; in making the stroke; when teeing the ball; in repairing damage to the green.* Let us look at those four exceptions with some care because this is another rule much abused by golfers at all levels.

In fairly taking your stance. The important word here is 'fairly' and you must be the judge of that. If your ball is in bushes you must clearly bend growing branches when you take your stance. What you must not do is wield your wedge like a machete and hack away inconvenient vegetation. Nor must you pull aside branches and trap them under your foot because that is not fairly taking a stance. You must not trample behind the ball, flattening the undergrowth for a clean shot at the ball. This is a favourite dodge of the golfing cheat. He positions his bag in such a way that when he addresses the ball and then changes his mind about the choice of club, his foot naturally comes down behind the ball as he steps across to make a new selection. After a few such changes of mind he can confidently get a straight-faced club to what had previously been a hopeless lie. A variation on this ploy is to stand beside the ball idly making practice swings in the pretence of total absorption in the difficulties of the shot but in reality hacking away inconvenient tuffets or saplings.

In the case of saplings and young trees, these are sometimes staked and the committee may make a local rule for a free drop clear of them. This is what happens in professional golf but the local rule providing relief is by no means universal. In any case, the purpose of such a local rule is for the protection of the tree, not for the benefit of the golfer. After all, the tree has been planted for the express purpose of providing interference to the wayward golfer and in due course the tree will be able to stand on its own feet without a stake. Wilful destruction of growing vegetation has no place in golf and if there is no local rule the thoughtful golfer will accept the penalty of declaring his ball unplayable (of which more later) than risk demolishing a young tree or shrub.

That injunction, which has nothing to do with the rules of golf, applies equally to the second exception, *in making the stroke.* When you swing the club you may well break or bend growing vegetation and provided it does not constitute the kind of vandalism mentioned above, that is perfectly all right.

The third exception, *when teeing the ball,* means in practice that you are free to tread firmly behind your teed ball to press down loose earth or grass. And the fourth exception, *on the green*, covers the repair of pitch marks, of which more anon. Having absorbed the intention behind this rule, it ought to be easy enough to remember two further provisions. You must not build a stance, such as by scraping up loose sand to create a level area; your only entitlement is to place your feet firmly (which includes a degree of shuffling and squirming). And if your ball is in long grass, or similar concealing conditions, you can only touch as much of it as to enable you to find and identify your ball. You must in no way improve its lie and the rules insist you have no divine right to a sight of your ball as you play the shot.

There has been one decision on the rules for improving the line of play which illuminates the philosophy underlying these regulations. A player whose ball was off the green wanted to use his putter but there was a puddle of water on the green in the line of his shot. He wanted a free drop to a position which would give him a water-free line to the hole but this request was quite properly refused because his ball was not on the green. The player therefore had his caddie mop up the puddle. The Rules of Golf Committee decreed that this was unlawful action to influence the movement of the ball.

PRACTICE STROKES AND SWINGS (7)

Some of the most straightforward rules cause the most trouble. Take the example of Rule 7 which simply states: *During the play of a hole, a player shall not play any practice stroke.* Remember that a *stroke* is defined as the forward movement of a club with the intention of hitting the ball. What could be easier to understand and remember? The reason for the rule is apparent; golf would be a much easier game if we could all play practice strokes and then, once we had found the best way of playing the shot by trial and error, we could say: 'O.K. This one is for real.' That would not be golf and the fact is so obvious that the rule is almost superfluous. This is not one of the rules which is wired into the golfer's mental alarm system because such hypersensitive precautions are not necessary. And there lies the danger. For instance, a competitor in a national amateur championship found an old ball in the rough. It had been badly

chewed by a dog, or fox, and was therefore absolutely useless for any purpose. Even the most impoverished enthusi-
ast would have rejected it as a gift for his practice bag. The
player remarked to his fellow competitor: 'There is only
one fate fit for this miserable specimen' and idly chipped it
into a lake. Most of us have done the same sort of thing
from time to time in social games. But this was a serious
competition and the golfer was guilty of playing a practice
stroke. He was duly penalised two strokes (in match-play
he would have lost the hole).

This is a good example of how the rules must be applied
literally, without regard for the most innocent of intentions.
So if you are held up on the course and must expend your
restless energy on swinging a club, make sure you do not
use a ball. It is perfectly all right to make practice swings,
swishing at daisies or thrashing the empty air, or even hitting acorns and chestnuts. And if you are making a practice
swing on the tee and, as sometimes happens, you smack the
club into the turf with such violence that the seismic vibra-
tions dislodge your ball from its tee-peg, that does not
count as a stroke since you had no intention to hit the ball.
But until you have completed the hole be sure not to hit
practice strokes of any kind. Once you have holed out, and
before starting to play the next hole, you are allowed to
while away the time (always provided you are not holding
up play) by replaying putts on the green you have just completed or trying to chip into the trash basket on the next
tee, or play practice shots provided you avoid two punishable offences: you must *not* make a practice stroke out of
any hazard and you must *not* play a practice stroke on – or
on to – any green except the one you have just completed.
The usual penalties apply – two strokes or loss of hole (the
next hole, that is, not the one just completed).

Of course, there is an obligation on every golfer to show
due consideration in this business of practice shots and
practice swings. It is inexcusable to gouge divots out of the
tee, or indeed the surrounds, as you swing away waiting for
your opportunity to start play at the next hole. Incidentally,
you should not replace divots on the tee, the one occasion
when the bleeding wound in the turf should be left open.
And it is equally uncouth to play practice shots which

might disturb another player. Championships have been lost by players inadvertently taking practice strokes, notably the New Zealand Open Championship of 1937. A former winner, A. Murray, was waiting for a fellow competitor to putt out before he himself could complete the hole and he absent-mindedly dropped his ball at the edge of the green and played a practice putt.

FOREIGN MATERIALS (4)

James Braid, the great Scottish champion, who ruled the roost of British golf for many years in company with Harry Vardon and J.H. Taylor as 'The Great Triumvirate', always carried a piece of chalk in his golf jacket. He advocated that in wet weather the face of the driver should be rubbed with chalk to dry the surface and give a better purchase on the ball to impart backspin. That was a common dodge among the professionals of the day but latterly the Rules of Golf Committee have clamped down on the addition of 'foreign material' to either ball or club during play for the purpose of changing their playing characteristics. So much for the wonder aerosol sprays which advertisers tell us will add yards to the flight of a golf ball. Even if true, such foreign material would be illegal. (You can *clean* clubs and ball, of course, because this is not intended to change their playing characteristics.)

That sounds like a straightforward rule, but it had one tragicomic consequence for the English tournament player, Guy Hunt, a smallish man who needs all the help he can get to achieve distance off the tee. He discovered that when his driver was wet it put less backspin on the ball, just as Braid had explained. But Hunt was not interested in backspin, which is what gives the ball a high, floating trajectory. He wanted distance and with a wet-faced driver his shots flew lower and, with more run, farther. He therefore fell into the habit of licking his thumb and wiping it over the face of his driver. It was Lee Trevino, the American multiple champion, who first alerted Hunt to the dangers of this practice. Hunt was thoroughly embarrassed at the thought that he might have been infringing a rule of golf and his form suffered badly. He wrote to the Royal and Ancient Golf Club at St Andrews for a ruling. Meanwhile Hunt experimented with different drivers and adjustments to his swing to improve his driving with a dry-faced club. In due course the R and A exonerated Hunt but later had second thoughts and decreed that spit on the driver was a foreign material added to change the club's playing characteristics. Fortunately, by now Hunt had returned to form and was driving well with his new spit-free method, so the decision did not bother him. That is a way-out example but if you are of an experimental turn of mind, you might, for instance, be tempted to add a piece of lead tape to your driver. If so, do not do it during a round because that most definitely would come under the heading of changing the character of the club during play.

ARTIFICIAL AIDS (14)

In the same spirit, the rules try to maintain the natural feeling of golf by banning artificial aids (under penalty of disqualification) such as range-finders, wind gauges and spirit levels for measuring the slopes on the green (all of which have been marketed from time to time). If you want to judge the speed and direction of the wind you are allowed to hold up a handkerchief or toss a few blades of grass into the air. As for judging distances you may well ask about those yardage charts which the professionals prepare for tournaments and which are increasingly available commercially for many courses. Well, the rules obviously permit their use although you should not dally too long pouring over your notes and pacing off from your markers. This could be held to be unduly delaying play.

People who need glasses are not infringing the rule against artificial aids but it is interesting to speculate on the subject. Glasses are normally made up for long sight or close work, or are combined as bifocals. Opticians can just as easily make up glasses focused on the exact distance between the eye in the address position and the ball. Such glasses are invaluable to players who naturally see an indistinct image of the ball they are addressing since the eye is the key to the whole series of reflex actions involved in the swing. Would such golf glasses, useless for any other purpose, be classified as an artificial device? It is impossible to anticipate the answer since no test case has yet been put to the Rules of Golf committees. On the one hand they seem to qualify as an artificial device under the rule but they also do no more than put the wearer on a par with normally sighted players. So they give no special advantage. All they do is enable a man with failing faculties to continue playing the game – but so did croquet putting, now outlawed (16). We shall have to wait to see the outcome of that one. Hand-warmers are legal, provided golfers use them to warm their hands and not their golf balls.

ARTIFICIAL AIDS WHAMMY

The golf magazines are a rich source of advertisements for golfing gadgetry 'guaranteed' to add yards and yards to your drive. You can take your choice of miracle clubs and balls, wonders of the latest space age technology whose guarantees will add at least 50 yards to your drive. Then there are patent socks and gloves and wrist bands and headgear and shoes and even tee pegs, all promising an extra ten yards or so. How is the average golfer to know whether such beguiling merchandise is legal? Well, the rule of thumb is that unless the advertisement carries a solemn declaration that the article in question has been approved by the Rules of Golf Committee, you can assume that the claim is a pack of lies, sheer fiction invented by a rather desperate copywriter. If you are of a gullible nature by all means purchase that over-priced glove with miracle weighting in the wrist-band because, although it may be artificial, by no stretch of the imagination could it be classified as an aid to golf. Such, you might feel, was the case with the golf shoes which the American professional, John Huston, was paid to endorse. The soles of these shoes were cunningly contoured to assist the weight shift during the swing, or so it was claimed. A zealous official – over-zealous, as you might feel – cautioned Huston that he would be disqualified if he availed himself of these artificial aids. Whammy! Huston had the last laugh. He bought a pair of conventional golf shoes in the pro's shop and went out and won the tournament. Reverse whammy.

BALL UNFIT FOR PLAY (5)

It is appropriate before leaving the subject of defective sight to cover one possible result of such infirmity, namely damage to that expensive golf ball. If your ball becomes so badly damaged that it is unfit for play, you may substitute another during play of the hole where the damage occurred and in the presence of your opponent or marker. That means that if you cut your ball on the second hole, you cannot suddenly decide to change it halfway up the fifth fairway. (You can change your ball at any time between holes, of course.) This is one of the rare occasions when you *place* a ball during play through the green instead of dropping. The idea is to give yourself the identical lie.

The rules have recently been expanded to clarify exactly what is meant by 'unfit for play'. It must be visibly damaged, by a cut, or crack or distortion, so as to interfere with its true flight or roll. Scratched paint is not enough to declare a ball unfit. Failure to comply with the correct procedure carries a penalty of one stroke. Mud sticking to your ball is patently not damage in this sense and cannot be said to have made the ball unfit to play. That is just bad luck. Can it be cleaned in any circumstances? Let us see.

CLEANING THE BALL

Very few golfers are totally confident about their rights in this business of when the ball may be cleaned. Some clean the ball every time they pick it up and often enough they get away with it because their opponents are not sure enough of their ground to exact the penalty. Others have a vague idea that cleaning is forbidden in some circumstances but, not being sure which these illegal instances might be, they never clean the ball and thus deny themselves a quite legitimate advantage. It is not a particularly important point in everyday, social golf but when competition days come around every golfer should make it a point of honour, not to say common sense, to observe every rule to the strict letter. After all, some of us can reflect ruefully on the day when we played and scored well, only to be denied a prize because of penalty strokes. It is only through such hard experiences that many golfers become aware of the more esoteric rules.

There are two occasions when you are allowed to clean your ball. The first is when you are *on the green* before each putt (16), although this right is thoroughly overdone and once should be enough on most occasions. Excessive ball cleaning is one of the main causes of slow play. The second occasion is *when you are taking relief* – that is to say, when lifting from an unplayable or embedded lie (28); when lifting from an obstruction; when lifting from ground under repair, burrowing animal scrapes or casual water; and when lifting from a water hazard.

It follows that you are *not* allowed to clean when lifting your ball to identify it, except by the minimum amount necessary to make the identification, when you have to mark and lift your ball through the green because it is interfering with someone else's stroke; and when you are replacing a ball which has been moved by an outside agency.

Perhaps it will help to clarify the rule to remember that if you are picking up your ball for any reason, you can clean it if you are putting it back into play in a different position; you cannot clean (except on the green) if replacing it in its original position.

The convention among professionals when they have to lift a ball on a cleaning-forbidden occasion is to pick it up between two extended fingers and then to hold it up rather ostentatiously to show that they are not doing a bit of unobtrusive rubbing with the thumb. Such flaunting of holiness may appear slightly rich for ordinary occasions, but at least it is preferable to an accusation of sneaking a surreptitious clean.

A word of caution is in order at this point on the method you use to restore your ball's pristine condition. By far the commonest practice is a quick lick and wipe of the ball on a towel, or, more likely, your shirt. This is not to be recommended because some highly toxic chemicals are used by greenkeepers, especially in control of worms, so licking golf balls can cause severe bellyache, or worse.

It may be asked why you should be allowed to clean your ball on one occasion and not on another. Some people go so far as to advocate that golfers should be permitted to clean a ball at any time, since mud on the ball makes it impossible to exercise full control over the shot. It would seem, therefore, that the rules favour the luck of the bounce rather than skill. That is exactly the case. In a cross-country game such as golf, the element of luck can never be eliminated entirely. The luck of the bounce, enshrined in the expression 'a rub of the green', has always been an integral part of golf and one of the functions of the modern custodians of the game's traditions is to retain the spirit of the game as best they may.

Over the years concessions have been grudgingly made about cleaning the ball but only to the extent of easing situations in which golf becomes unplayable. It sometimes happens, for instance, that when you play from a particularly glutinous lie the ball sticks to the club face. It has been ruled in that case that the rule of equity operates. You pick the ball off the club face and drop it, without penalty, as near as possible to its original lie. Then you have another go, but you do not clean the ball in the meantime. You are stuck with the mud, and vice versa.

But you could have elected to declare your ball unplayable in the first place. If you had done so you would have had to pay for it, and the lawmakers, in their infinite charity, have decreed that a wipe of the ball is part of the bargain for your payment of a penalty stroke. Golf offers many dilemmas as to which option you should most prudently select and part of the skill of the game lies in making a wise choice.

Having made provision to clean the ball in taking relief from an unplayable ball, it is a matter of consistency to allow cleaning when obtaining relief for other reasons, whether free or under penalty. As for cleaning on the green, often a ball arrives on the putting surface in a totally unputtable condition. For a time there was a rule that you could clean your ball once only on the green but that legislation was rescinded, and now you can clean on the green as often as you like.

3 | PENALTIES

TWO STROKE PENALTIES

Before examining the troublesome situations in which a golfer may find himself, let us look at the philosophy of golf penalties. Many golfers are confused over the scale of penalties and even after years of experience they are still unsure about which situations call for a two stroke penalty and those which carry only one stroke. Generally speaking, the two shot penalty, or loss of hole in match-play, is the punishment for a player accidentally breaking a rule of golf. (Deliberate breaking of rules, or cheating, is always punishable by disqualification.) So all those mishaps like playing a wrong ball, or shanking and hitting your own golf bag with your ball, or having your putt hit the flagstick, incur the standard two stroke penalty.

ONE STROKE PENALTIES

One stroke penalties are not really punishments. They are in two categories, the first of which we might think of in terms of prices. For example, if your ball is in a bush you have to decide whether to have a hack at it or whether it is worth the price of declaring it unplayable and dropping clear. In that case you are exercising your right to lift and drop at the cost of one stroke. In effect, you are buying your way out of trouble. The same principle applies to the case of having your ball land in casual water in a bunker. You have to ask yourself whether to take a free drop in the bunker or whether it is a worthwhile bargain to 'spend' a penalty stroke on the right to drop the ball outside the hazard. The other class of one stroke penalties are 'ghost' strokes. The rules of golf say in effect that if your ball is moved accidentally, perhaps as you were picking up a loose twig, then that is the same as if you had moved it with a club. So that's a stroke. In the same way, an air shot is a ghost stroke, in its effect on the ball. But you intended to hit the ball and must count the stroke. Another common ghost stroke is when you address the ball and it moves as you ground the club. Now we have to be absolutely precise at this point. It is quite common for the ball to move slightly when it is addressed, notably with a putter, and it is up to the conscience of the golfer to identify the type of movement. If the ball simply rocks slightly and settles back in exactly its original position, then no penalty is involved. But if the ball moves, if only by a fraction, and comes to rest in a new position, then the rules (18) say that is one penalty stroke, except when addressing the ball on the tee, and the ball must be replaced.

It often happens that a ball sitting in the rough will move when addressed by a club; the act of placing the club-head by the ball disturbs the grass and the ball is dislodged. That is why many professionals and good amateurs make a point of never grounding their clubs in the rough. By keeping the club-head clear of the grass, they do not risk accidentally causing the ball to move. What is more, if the ball should happen to move anyway, perhaps through the spontaneous collapse of supporting grasses, they are still in the clear because technically they are not at the address. Under the rules, a player is in the address position when he has taken his stance and has grounded the club behind the ball. (In a hazard you are at the address position as soon as you take up your stance because you are not allowed to ground your club in hazards.)

UNPLAYABLE LIE (28)

Many golfers look on the rules as a series of prohibitions and penalties set to trap them and punish their innocent mistakes. In fact, the rules can be allies as well as enemies and one of the most important examples of the rules as the golfer's Bill of Rights is the unplayable lie concession. We have already seen how the principle of the ghost stroke works.

If you accidentally move your ball, such as by inadvertently kicking it during a search or starting it to roll by moving a dead twig, then the rules say, in effect, that this is the same as if you had moved the ball with a club and you therefore add a penalty shot to your score (18). Now the same principle is extended to allow you to do the same thing deliberately by 'paying' a stroke. The first thing to remember is that it is your decision to declare your ball unplayable. It can be in a perfect lie in the centre of the fairway if you like. It is up to you and no one can question your right to declare your ball unplayable at any time, or in any place (except in a water hazard) even on the green. In practice, of course, you use this device only when your ball is in a fairly desperate situation and you feel it to be a bargain to extricate it.

If you do decide to declare your ball unplayable there are three courses you can follow for the price of your penalty stroke. First, you can follow the stroke-and-distance procedure by going back to the spot from which you played the previous shot. If that happened to be a tee shot, then you are at liberty to tee-up your ball again. Otherwise you drop the ball or, if on the green, you place it.

The second option is to drop the ball within two club-lengths but not nearer the hole. The ball can now roll another two club-lengths quite legitimately without needing to be re-dropped. Indeed, you would incur a penalty if you picked it up, because it is now in play. Great care should always be taken when dropping a ball because it can happen that having paid your penalty and taken an unplayable ball drop, the ball can roll into more trouble. The Rules of Golf Committee was asked to give a decision on the case of a player who declared his ball unplayable and took a drop only to have the ball roll against a tree trunk. It was within the legal limit and not nearer the hole. He felt that he should get another drop, without penalty, as he had already paid to get relief from an unplayable lie. Not at all, ruled the wise men. The player had three options under the unplayable ball rule and having taken the risk of the two club-lengths process, he must face the consequences. Therefore he must either play the ball as it lay against the tree or declare it unplayable again with another penalty stroke.

The third action you can take is to drop the ball as far as you like behind the spot where you declared it unplayable, keeping that spot between you and the hole. It is extremely important to be clear on that last point as it is one of the most abused procedures in golf. One of the commonest situations for invoking the unplayable lie rule occurs when you hit into trees at the side of the fairway and your ball ends up against a tree trunk or in a bush. In that case many golfers who are not thoroughly conversant with the rule and simply have a hazy notion that you can drop as far back along the line as you like, assume that this means the line along which the ball entered the woods. They therefore go back towards the tee, or towards the spot where they played the last shot, and drop the ball as soon as they are in the clear. That is quite wrong. If you are in woods such as those we have been discussing, then the correct procedure – keeping the point of the unplayable lie between you and the hole – would take you deeper into the woods. So get the provisions of this rule absolutely clear in your mind and save yourself the embarrassment of being accused of trying to take unfair advantage. The rules try to be fair and the golfer who tries to follow that same precept of fairness will not go far wrong. On that basis it should be easy enough to remember that if you declare your ball unplayable in a bunker, then you have the universal remedy of stroke and distance but if you choose either of the other two procedures, dropping sideways or back along the line, then the ball must be dropped in the bunker. A ball in a water hazard may not be declared unplayable.

Now let us look at some unusual situations where the unplayable ball rules can be used. What if your ball gets stuck up a tree? Well, Arnold Palmer had that problem in Australia and he chose to climb the tree and play the ball, which he did with remarkable success. But that kind of adventurous behaviour is not recommended. In climbing the tree you might dislodge the ball (penalty stroke) and if it fell against the tree trunk, you would have to declare it unplayable (another penalty stroke). Better to declare it unplayable before touching the tree. Now you can dislodge it in any way you like. But, you say, what if the ball was more than one club-length above the ground – how could it be dropped? That problem has been covered by the legislators; you measure your two club-lengths from the point directly below where your ball lodged. An appeal was once made over the case of a player who climbed a tree. His weight caused considerable movement of the trunk in which his ball was lodged but it remained securely wedged in a fork. The question now arose whether he was guilty of moving his ball. Although the ball was clearly in motion, the committee decided that no penalty was called for since the ball did not move in relation to its surroundings.

BALL OUT OF BOUNDS (27)

If you clearly see your ball go out of bounds then the procedure is simple. You apply the stroke-and-distance rule by going back to the place from which you played the last shot.

You are already rooted to the spot in all probability, hopping from foot to foot and cursing your bad luck. You drop another ball (tee it up if on the tee) and add a penalty stroke. That means in the case of a drive that your next tee shot will be your third stroke – in common golfing parlance 'hitting three off the tee'.

BOUNDARIES

The difficulties arise when you are not sure if your ball is out of bounds. It is the club's duty to define its boundaries and explicit details should be provided with the local rules on the back of the score card. But problems do arise in borderline cases and one of them should be noted because it is at variance with what you might expect from your knowledge of common law. Where fences are used to mark a boundary, it is common practice to string the fence wire, or nail the runners, on the outside limit of the property, or the far side of the posts. In golf the boundary is always the line drawn between the inside limits of the posts and you are out of bounds when all of your ball is over that line. Thus there is a strip of no man's land the thickness of the posts which is out of bounds for golfers but nevertheless is within the boundaries of the club. If a trench is used to define out of bounds, as along the top of the famous Cops of Royal Liverpool, the trench itself is out of bounds. And when a line is drawn to mark the boundary, the line is out of bounds. But there is nothing to stop you standing out of bounds to play a ball which is in bounds.

LOST BALL (27)

Now the matter becomes slightly complicated, but so long as we keep the principle of stroke-and-distance in mind, then it will make the alternative procedures all the easier to remember. You see your ball disappear from sight into an area where there is a good chance it will be lost. Forget about water hazards for the moment, which are governed by a special procedure which will be explained later. For the present let us stick with the other manifold opportunities for losing a ball. If you see it heading for an area where you think it may be lost, here is what you do. You either formally abandon it and put another ball into play or you announce that you propose to play a provisional ball and, if on the tee, you tee up another ball and hit it, after everyone else has driven off. If necessary, you go on playing that provisional ball until you reach the area where you think your original may be. Now, on arrival at the search area, there are two things to be done: announce clearly to everyone helping in the hunt the brand and number on your ball; and take note of the time. You are allowed five minutes to hunt for a ball and at this point you wave through any players who are waiting behind.

This business of calling through players behind you is one of the most important courtesies in golf and sadly it is becoming more and more neglected. There are few greater frustrations than to be held up during a round while the players in front search for a ball. If your ball cannot be found within the five minute limit then it is officially lost and you continue the hole, playing your provisional ball under the stroke-and-distance rule. That is to say, you count the original shot from which the first ball was lost, plus one penalty stroke and all the strokes played with the provisional ball. If the original ball is found you play on with it, and simply pick up your provisional ball, without penalty.

It is important to bear in mind that the provisional ball procedure is not a device which allows you a choice of how you will play the hole according to the way things work out. For example, if you walk forward and find your original ball and it is in a desperate lie, you cannot say: 'I deem that ball lost and I will continue play with the provisional.' Facts are facts and if your ball is found then that is the ball in play. You must continue with it and pick up the provisional or declare the ball unplayable.

That second option creates another pitfall for the unwary in the matter of provisional balls. Suppose that you hit a shot from which you believe your ball may be lost, and you play a provisional ball. Now you find the original ball in a hopeless lie and decide to declare it unplayable. One of your options in this case is stroke and distance but, you reason, you have already followed the stroke and distance procedure in playing that provisional ball. Why not add a penalty stroke and play on with the provisional? That would be unlawful, because a provisional ball may only be used in the case of a lost ball. Your ball is not lost so, if you elect on stroke and distance, you must go back to where you played the previous stroke.

PROVISIONAL BALL (27)

This use of a provisional ball is simply a device to save time: it is intended that if you have to apply the stroke-and-distance rule you do not have the bother of walking all the way back. Of course there will be many times when you have no advance inkling that your ball will be lost or out of bounds. You have driven off and walk forward confidently but when you get up there you can see no sign of the ball. You call the match behind through and search for five minutes without success. Now you have no option but to go back to where you played the last shot and play under the stroke-and-distance rule. There is absolutely no way of avoiding that long walk back, which can be highly embarrassing on a crowded course, and so it is a good idea always to play a provisional ball if there is the slightest chance that your original ball may be lost or OB. After all, it does not cost anything in the way of penalties to play a provisional ball and you get more golf for your money.

SECOND BALL (3)

There is another occasion on which the playing of another ball can be used to save time and argument and wear on the nervous system. In stroke-play only, if a knotty point of golf law should arise (and even if you learn this book by heart there will be occasions when you are unsure how to proceed) you may find yourself at odds with your companions. Someone will perhaps say that you can have a free drop but you yourself, by now hopefully a firm devotee to the play-it-as-it-lies principle, will be unsure that this suggestion is firmly founded on the rules. After all, there are very few golfers who are thoroughly familiar with every nuance of every rule although many are prepared to put forward their misguided judgements with confidence. For instance, it may be felt that your ball is in a place which is possibly ground under repair, or affected by an obstruction, or borderline casual water. If there is any doubt, follow both courses of action (3). Play the original ball as it lies and take his suggestion by dropping a second ball as well in the place suggested by the doubtful rule. Announce clearly to your marker which ball you wish to count, provided the committee approves your procedure. Play out the hole with both balls and when you complete the round, unless you have made the same score with both balls, put the problem to the committee for a ruling before you sign your card. If the committee rules that the nominated ball was put into play in accordance with the rules the score with that ball shall count. You can only use this alternative ball procedure in stroke-play. (In a match every dispute must be settled on the hole where it occurs.)

Before moving on from the problem of a lost ball, we should examine some of the difficulties we may meet during the actual five minute search. One possibility is that you may take one horrified look at the area into which you saw your ball disappear and decide that it is hopeless even to begin looking for it. In that case you can declare the ball unplayable and proceed under the stroke-and-distance rule. Suppose you plunge into the undergrowth and snarl 'This is hopeless' and fight your way back to the fairway. And suppose that now your opponent, who we may assume has sportingly gone into the jungle with you calls out: 'Hello here's a ball. What were you playing, a Dunlop 4? Oh what bad luck that you had already abandoned it. Really it's not lying too badly at all.'

Well, had you abandoned it? The rules of golf state that a ball cannot become lost by a declaration. So what about that procedure of declaring the ball unplayable? Well the original ball does not become lost at the moment of your declaration, only when you put another ball into play, by the act of dropping it or by striking it off the tee.

A revealing example of the dangers inherent in this situation was provided in the British Open Championship of 1974 at Royal Lytham. The South African Dale Hayes hit into the wild, scrubby rough which is such a feature of linksland courses and after a short while (well inside his five minutes' grace) he left his fellow competitors to continue the search while he went back to the place from which he had played the shot. In effect, he was saving time and showing due consideration for golfers following behind, because he would now be ready to continue under the stroke-and-distance rule the moment his five minutes expired. He dropped another ball but before he played it – and still within his five minutes – a shout from the search area told him his original ball had been found. With a great feeling of relief he picked up the second ball and returned to play his original. He was later penalised because the moment he dropped another ball he legally abandoned his 'lost' ball and the second ball became the one in play. So the dropping of a ball is the vital act of abandonment, not the addressing or striking of it.

A number of misconceptions have grown up about how a player can abandon his ball. Many people believe that once you turn your back on the search area you have abandoned your ball. That is rubbish. Your ball can become lost only in one of three ways: if it is not found after searching for five minutes, or by the act of putting another ball into play, or by continuing play with your provisional ball beyond the point where your original ball is likely to be lost.

BALL MOVED (18)

Another danger of the hunt is that while you are thrashing about in the vegetation, you may very well accidentally move your ball. It is no use complaining that you didn't mean it and that where there is no guilty intention there can be no crime. The high principles of Roman law have no precedence in the rules of golf, and accidentally moving the ball, either directly or causing it to move by touching anything (such as a fallen branch), comes into the category of our ghost strokes. You must add a penalty stroke to your score and replace the ball.

The same procedure applies if your partner or either of your caddies moves your ball accidentally during a search: take your penalty and replace the ball.

However, if an opponent, or a fellow competitor in stroke-play, or their caddies, or anyone not involved in the game, accidentally moves your ball there is no penalty and the ball must be replaced by you. It should be carefully noted that we are talking about accidentally moving a ball *during a search.* If a ball is accidentally moved in general play, a different set of rules apply but the principles remain the same.

Now, if your ball is accidentally moved by a match-play opponent, his caddie or equipment, then no penalty is involved and you must replace the ball.

How strictly should this rule about accidentally moving a ball during a search be observed? If you are hunting in deep rough and inadvertently move your ball half an inch, or dislodge it from a precarious perch on a tuffet, does it really demand a penalty stroke? That is a question for each golfer to answer for himself, just one of the many occasions in golf when the player must be guided by his own conscience. However, there is one common mishap which often occurs during a search and which clearly causes the ball to move within the strict meaning of the rule. That is when you find the ball by stepping on it. You feel that welcome bulge under your foot and shout 'Here's a ball.' Now while the ball nearly always moves by becoming further embedded into the turf, this is one occasion when most people agree that no penalty is warranted. Mind you, the rules of golf do not sanction this custom. The rules mean what they say. But in stepping on a ball, while it is obviously depressed, there is no way of determining that it did not revert to its original position when the weight of your foot was removed.

So let us agree to an unofficial compact to penalise ourselves if we kick the ball but not simply if we step on it.

IDENTIFYING BALL (12)

Before we play on we must make sure that it really is our ball. Provided the ball is not in a hazard, this is one of the rare occasions when it is permissible to lift and replace the ball. However, it can only be done for the purposes of identifying it (no wholesale cleaning, of course) and it must be done in the presence of your opponent or fellow competitor. The reason for the independent witness is to guarantee the next proviso: that the ball is replaced in its exact position. If it is buried up to its waist in mud it must go back like that with no hanky panky about surreptitiously improving the lie under the guise of identifying it.

WRONG BALL (15)

It is important to identify your ball beyond doubt because there are harsh penalties to be paid for playing a wrong ball. These in themselves are an excellent reason for getting into the habit of carefully inspecting your ball before every shot – even when there is no possibility of doubt that it is yours. Obviously you do not lift to make this routine identification; you would become a highly suspicious character if you did that kind of thing, even though you were acting within the laws. But the habit of scrutinising your ball carefully on every shot saves you from the risk of playing a wrong ball and also helps your golf in that you absorb the details of its lie more thoroughly, and therefore produce the appropriate shot.

In match-play, if by chance you should happen to play a wrong ball (except in a hazard) you lose the hole. Your only hope of reprieve is if your opponent has also played a wrong ball and you can mutually determine that he played a wrong ball first. In that case he lost the hole. And in those cases where players accidentally exchange balls during the play of a hole and they cannot discover who played a wrong ball first, then the hole must be played out with the exchanged balls.

In stroke-play, if you play a wrong ball (again, except in a hazard) you add a two stroke penalty and then play your correct ball. Strokes played with the wrong ball do not count and if it happens to belong to a fellow competitor, it must be replaced. Of course, you may not notice that you have been playing a wrong ball until you hole out. Well, provided you have not hit off on the next tee, you can still follow the wrong-ball procedure, provided you can be sure of where you started to play the wrong ball. If you do not discover the error until you are playing the next hole (or have left the 18th green in the case of the last hole) then you must disqualify yourself because you have not completed the stipulated round in accordance with the rules.

BUNKERS AND WATER HAZARDS (26)

If you are in a hazard then you cannot lift your ball to identify it. All you can do if your ball is buried in loose sand, or under leaves, or such like, is to brush aside enough sand or other debris to determine that there is a golf ball of some kind down there. As soon as you detect a speck of white synthetic rubber, you have to stop. You have no divine right to a clear sight of your ball at any time in golf; you are only entitled to know the site of it. That applies everywhere but in a hazard it does not matter because in this one instance there is no penalty for playing a wrong ball. If you splash out of a bunker and discover that it wasn't your ball you played, you can go right back into the hazard and go on hitting any balls that you see until such time as you hit your own (15). That just about wraps up the lost-ball situation. If it can't be found after a five minute search, or if you decide to abandon it as lost anyway, you either go back and play another under the stroke-and-distance rule or you continue play with your provisional ball if you have had the foresight to put one into play.

The one exception to these lost-ball procedures is if you hit one into a water hazard. There are two types of water hazard – ordinary and lateral – and they should be clearly defined in the local rules on the card of the course. So if you see your ball go into the water, the first thing to do is consult the card and discover if you are in ordinary water or lateral water. Mind you, your ball need not necessarily be immersed in water. Perhaps it is embedded in a bank or has disappeared down a deep fissure in the cracked mud of a pond which has not seen a drop of water for months. That makes no difference. If the local rule says it is water then water it is, wet or dry, and if your ball is within the defined boundaries of the hazard, you are in water. Of course, you may play the ball as it lies but, being in a hazard, you must not ground your club or remove any loose impediments. But let us assume that your ball is hopelessly immersed in water.

With an ordinary water hazard you can proceed under the stroke-and-distance rule or you can take advantage of the one genuinely humane piece of legislation in the rule book. Not that compassion was the guiding motive behind the legislation. Never mind. Let us not question the motives too deeply just now. What you do is drop a ball, under penalty of one stroke, keeping the spot where the shot last crossed its boundary between you and the hole. You can go as far back along that line as you like. In practice, of course, the most usual case is to drop as near to the water as possible so as to give yourself the shortest shot on your second attempt to carry the water.

Now we have the lateral water hazards which are usually ponds and ditches running roughly in the same direction as the line of play. Here you have the same two options as for a ball lost in an ordinary water hazard and another possibility as well. You can drop under penalty of one stroke within two club-lengths of *either* side of the hazard opposite the point where the shot last crossed its boundary.

Finally, the ball may be lost in a hazard – and now we are talking about regular bunkers, not water hazards – in which there is an accumulation of casual water, snow, ground under repair, or scrapes caused by a burrowing animal. In that case you can drop another ball in the hazard *without penalty* (26) in an area which avoids interference from these special conditions either to your ball or your stance. Alternatively you can drop behind the hazard under penalty of one stroke.

Under a recent revision you are no longer entitled to relief in a water hazard from depredations made by a burrowing animal or from immovable obstructions. The lawmakers who added these refinements were clearly not regular visitors to Penina on the Portuguese Algarve coast where the banks of some water hazards are pock-marked by the holes of water rats but, as I have observed earlier, hazards are supposed to be hazardous. The immovable obstruction alteration is a good one because it eliminates all arguments about whether bridge supports and artificially surfaced banks are obstructions within the hazard or integral parts of the course.

The Rules of Golf provide relief for a ball embedded in its own pitch mark, a provision previously covered only in local rules. Now, if your ball plugs on the fairway, or on ground where the grass is cut to fairway length, such as the surrounds of a short hole, you may lift it without penalty, clean it (following the principle that the ball may always be cleaned when taking relief) and drop it. However, in one important particular this rule is at variance with established precedent. In every other case when taking relief, from ground under repair or casual water, for instance, you determine the nearest point which provides maximum relief from these conditions and then drop the ball within one club-length of that spot. In the case of a plugged ball, you must drop *as near as possible* to the pitch mark, not nearer the hole.

BUILDING A STANCE WHAMMY

The word 'stance' is firmly associated with standing and placing of the feet and so the golfer, who is forbidden by the rules to build himself a stance, naturally assumes that this prohibition is limited to improving the area on which he proposes to plonk his Footjoys. Accordingly, this rule did not cross the mind of the American Ryder Cup player, Craig Stadler, as he prepared to extricate his ball from beneath a bush. This necessitated kneeling down to play his shot and, the grass being damp and he being fastidious about complying with the PGA Tour's exhortation to competitors to present a neat and tidy public appearance, he first laid his towel on the ground. He now knelt and played his shot. When news of this incident reached the ears of the official referee he could scarcely credit what he was hearing. Such perfidy! The full penalty prescribed by law was visited upon the hapless Stadler. Whammy! Locker-room lawyers may care to discuss whether, in such circumstances, the donning of waterproof trousers would have constituted building a stance.

4 | INTERFERENCE

Outside Agencies

Golf courses are agreeable places, often quiet havens of greenery in industrial areas. They attract casual visitors who are there for purposes other than golf – to picnic, to stroll about enjoying the scenery, in the case of small boys to search for golf balls, and sometimes, notably when the course is part of a public park, for reasons which need not be too closely discussed here. By the same token, golf courses often teem with all manner of wildlife. Indeed, one of the beneficial effects of golf is that courses serve as nature reserves where threatened species of bird, insect and animal life can flourish free of the growing dangers from poisonous agricultural pesticides.

For the golfer, however, these various forms of extraneous humanity and natural life are classified under the general heading of 'outside agency'. It is a dull and unimaginative expression to describe the full spectrum of mankind and wildlife, but there it is. If a rare golden eagle swoops down and snatches your ball in mid-flight you, as a golfer, must suppress your ornithological excitement as best you may and think in terms of an outside agency. The author once watched in dismay while playing in the Danish Open Championship in Copenhagen as his ball was eaten by an outside agency in the form of a large red deer. Outside agencies can also be inanimate. A fellow competitor's golf ball can be an outside agency, as can a stray football kicked on to the course, and as too are spectators, referees, markers, fellow competitors and their caddies. The official definition describes an outside agency as *any agency not part of the match or, in stroke-play, not part of the competitor's side.*

The reason we must be quite sure of our grounds in recognising outside agencies is that they frequently affect our golf and it is important that the player should know what to do if his ball is carried off by a playful dog, or lands in a greenkeeper's pocket, or collides with another competitor's ball in mid-air.

BALL AT REST MOVED

The general rule through the green is that if your ball is stationary when it is moved by an outside agency you replace it. There is no penalty, of course, because the movement of the ball was none of your doing.

MOVING BALL STOPPED OR DEFLECTED

If your ball is moving when it is deflected or stopped by an outside agency, then you play it from where it comes to rest. Sometimes that is not possible, If your moving ball lodges in a moving outside agency, such as the talons of that golden eagle or the jaws of a dog, then obviously you cannot play it as it lies. In that event you drop a ball, without penalty, as near as you can judge to be the place where the outside agency took your ball. The procedure is different on the green. If a ball played on the green is in motion when it is stopped or deflected by an outside agency then that stroke is cancelled and the ball is replaced.

STATIONARY BALL

Confusion over the difference between the procedures for outside agencies influencing stationary and moving balls cost the South African Bobby Cole dearly in the British Open Championship at Hoylake in 1967. His ball had come to rest in a good lie near the green and a spectator running to get a good vantage point to watch the next shot kicked it into thick rough. Cole was not sure what to do about it so he relied on his instincts for sportsmanship and the spirit of the game. He had been brought up in the tradition that the ball must be played as it lies and so he felt that the safest thing to do was to play it from the long grass. It was a horribly difficult shot and cost him his par. Then, to make matters worse, he was penalised two strokes for not replacing his ball. Instead of a likely 4, or possible birdie 3, he ended up with a 7 for that hole.

As in the Tony Jacklin incident with the rabbit hole discussed in the introduction, Cole paid a high price for relying on his sense of sportsmanship. Incidentally, if an outside agency such as the spectator in the Bobby Cole incident moves your stationary ball, he is the best witness as to where it should be replaced. By all means let him point out the spot, but do not let him do the replacing. The rule requires the player to replace his ball and, as we have seen, in the rules of golf *every* word means what it says.

So much for the rules governing outside agencies. Now let us consider some of the cases when your ball is moved or deflected by what we may describe as inside agencies, even if the rules of golf disdain to use such an expression.

Inside Agencies

For our purposes here, inside agencies are people or equipment who are directly involved in our game of golf, either as partners, opponents, caddies and equipment. Note that a fellow competitor in a stroke-play event is not an inside agency. He is really nothing to do with you and counts as an outside agency if your ball is deflected by him or if he accidentally moves your ball. There is one important exception to that rule on the green and we will come to that later. For the moment we are concerned with play from tee to green and everything in this section will be concerned with play through the green. Some of the points have already been discussed in earlier sections, but no matter; a little repetition may help to make the lessons stick.

Stroke-play

First, let us look at inside agencies in stroke-play because the rules are simple (19). If your moving ball hits yourself (in a rebound for example) or your partner or either of your caddies or equipment, you suffer a penalty of two strokes. That's fair enough. After all, you have every control over your part of the game and it is clearly your fault if you hit anything. There is also a darker intention behind this rule. An unscrupulous caddie or partner could 'accidentally' deflect your shot to your advantage. Hence the dire penalty of two strokes. In the same way, if an outside agency or fellow competitor should 'accidentally' move your stationary ball there is no penalty. You replace your ball and play on. Now for a brief résumé of the procedures to follow if your stationary ball is moved, in both match- and stroke-play.

- By an outside agency. Replace it with no penalty.
- During a search by an opponent, fellow competitor or their caddies: replace it. No penalty
- By yourself, partner or your caddies, or by touching any-

thing which causes the ball to move: one penalty stroke and replace it.

- After you have addressed the ball except on tee: one penalty stroke and replace it.
- In touching a loose impediment within a club-length of your ball: one penalty stroke and replace it.

Match-play

In match-play the rules are slightly different and the best way to remember the distinction is to bear in mind the possibilities which could be provoked by the murkier depths of human nature in the heat of battle. If your moving ball is stopped or deflected by your opponent (or his caddie or equipment) there is no penalty but you can see to it that he gets no advantage from the mishap. You have the choice either to play the ball as it lies, a useful option if you have shanked an approach and the ball rebounds kindly off his head onto the green, or to cancel the stroke and replay it. In that case you *place* the ball on the spot where it lay previously, not drop it, because the intention is to give you the identical shot all over again. That procedure, which replaced the old loss-of-hole penalty for the opponent, should be sufficient to deter him from 'accidentally' getting in the way of one of your brilliant shots. But if we ascribe such dubious motives to the enemy, then we must assume ourselves to be capable of stooping just as low – as, for example, placing our golf bag in such a position to prevent the possibility of a ball rolling into a bunker. Therefore, if your ball hits anything to do with you – your own person, your partner, your caddies or your equipment – then you lose the hole.

We have already gone over the possibilities and procedures when you move your stationary ball. If your opponent (caddie and equipment) accidentally moves your stationary ball, he suffers a penalty stroke and you replace your ball.

The only exception to all this is the rare instance when your ball hits and moves your opponent's ball (remember, we are not yet on the green). In that case, there is no penalty, which neatly disposes of the dastardly possibility that when your balls lay close together you could knock yours against his and claim the hole. Bad luck, they've thought of that one. So there is no penalty. The moved ball must be replaced and the other ball played as it lies. If two balls in motion collide both must be played where they lie.

Outside agencies often intervene on big occasions when the course is swarming with spectators. Some golfers deliberately overhit their approaches to the greens which are screened at the back by solid walls of human flesh, confident of a rebound from shin or foot. At the US Masters at Augusta, a large bank behind the 18th green makes a natural grandstand and it is a favourite place for spectators to sit and watch the play. One year an approach shot rolled up the skirt of a woman who was sitting by the green. She jumped up and disappeared into the crowd with the ball still lodged on her person. Since the golfer was patently unable to play the ball from where it came to rest, an official awarded a free drop.

One outside agency which played a vital part in a competition was a lamb. During a club tournament at Burton-on-Trent in 1928 a competitor's ball was rolling up the edge of the green when the lamb picked it up in its mouth and neatly deposited it into the hole. But what are we to make of the case in which at the moment a player's ball dropped into the hole a large frog jumped out, knocking the ball out with it? The answer to that one is a question of fact according to Definition: *A ball is 'holed' when it lies within the circumference of the hole and all of it is below the level of the lip of the hole.*

DROPPING THE BALL

We have already touched on some of the occasions when a golfer may have to put a ball into play by dropping it. Dropping is a common experience for golfers and before going on to consider other occasions when dropping may be needed, we might pause briefly over the actual procedure of dropping. (Remember the general rule that when putting a ball into play you may tee it up if you are on the teeing ground; you drop it through the green or in a hazard; and you place it on the green.)

The procedure for dropping a ball sounds deceptively simple. You stand up straight holding the ball at shoulder height and drop it. There is no restriction on the direction the player faces. If the ball touches any part of the golfer or his clothing, before or after it strikes the ground, it must be re-dropped without penalty. That proviso, incidentally, solved the dilemma of the golfer who was wearing an anorak and under the old rule dropped his ball into the hood. Once it is on the ground, with the exceptions that we shall look at in a moment, it is in play.

In cases where relief is being taken keeping the hole and the site of the lifted ball in line (as from water hazards, abnormal ground conditions or unplayable lie), the ball must be dropped on that line. It is no longer permissible to drop the ball an arm's length to either side.

The nature of the occasions on which a player has to drop his ball often means that it is rough undulating territory and the ball frequently rolls away. It is here that for once the golfer's instinct for fair play can betray him. Usually in golf a player will not go far wrong if he abides by the common-sense solution to his dilemma but in dropping a ball it may roll a few feet into a much more favourable position. The golfer who tells himself that he is now taking an unfair advantage from a lucky bounce and re-drops his ball is in trouble. Unless the ball has rolled nearer the hole, it is in play *within two club-lengths of the point where it landed* and the moment the player touches that ball he is liable to a penalty.

The fair-play convention applies in all other cases. For example, if you are dropping a ball in a hazard and it rolls out, you re-drop in the hazard. Hard luck. But you may be dropping and see your ball roll into a hazard. Apply the common-sense solution and re-drop without penalty outside the hazard. The same applies to a ball rolling out of bounds. Re-drop. Sometimes the ground is so uneven that the ball would not come to rest within the permitted area if you went on dropping it all day. In that case, after trying two drops, you can place the ball in the correct position.

To summarise, there are four situations in which you must re-drop without penalty: if the ball touches you or your equipment during dropping; if it rolls nearer the hole; if it rolls more than two club-lengths from its point of impact; if it rolls out of bounds or into a hazard (or out of a hazard if this is where you are trying to drop it).

The situation to impress firmly on the mind is that one about club-lengths because many golfers are confused as to their rights. Say you are entitled to a free drop from a rabbit hole. You drop one club-length clear of the nearest point of relief from the rabbit hole and your ball can roll a further two club-lengths away, making a possible relief of three club-lengths in all.

A further complication can arise in dropping. Say a player has taken a drop from an unplayable lie and on dropping his ball it rolls less than two club-lengths but into ground under repair or behind an immovable obstruction. Well, the answer is simply to follow the logic of the situation. The drop was correctly performed and the ball is in play so now the golfer can take relief with another drop, possibly in quite a different place, under the rules governing ground under repair or obstructions. However, with the best will in the world it sometimes happens that a player drops, or places, his ball under an appropriate rule and then, after he has played his next shot, discovers that the drop, or placing, was in the wrong place. That mishap carries the standard penalty of two strokes or loss of hole.

BURROWING ANIMALS

The golfer is a lonely creature. He is not a member of a team with comrades to encourage and help him. He is all by himself with nothing but his own resources to fight the good fight against the tyrant golf ball. But if the golfer can look to no man for help (except from his caddie, if he has one, and even then the assistance must be limited to advice and encouragement), he may often find an ally among the dumb creatures of the field. So never scorn the snake in the grass, or the rabbit, or the delicate sandpiper which builds its nest by tunnelling into the ground. If your ball should come to rest in a hole or scrape or pile of earth made by such burrowing animals, or indeed if your stance or swing is affected by such natural inconveniences, then you can drop your ball clear within one club-length of the nearest point of relief (not nearer the hole of course) without penalty (25). In a bunker, you drop as near as possible to where the ball lay or, under penalty of one stroke, outside the bunker.

Once again a word of caution must be sounded. The rules here are, as always, to be taken literally. Birds, reptiles and burrowing animals mean exactly that and no more, and does not include the whole range of fauna.

And that is bad luck on golfers who play in tropical climates where ants abound and may build vast cathedrals 10ft high. The rules of golf give relief from loose granules of earth of normal anthills but not these solidly embedded tropical structures. Normally relief from such anthills is provided by a local rule but if not the only course is to fall back on the unplayable-ball rule (28) and spend a penalty stroke or to take courage in both hands, play the ball as it lies, and risk a multiple injection of formic acid from an army of maddened ants.

In some places the anthill also commonly does double-duty as the home of the king cobra and an injudicious blow with your wedge could provoke a situation which might test the loyalty of your friends to the limit. Always remember that the Rules of Golf give relief from situations which might involve physical danger. Play from a spot of equal difficulty and distance.

GROUND UNDER REPAIR

Exactly the same rules cover ground under repair and casual water. Ground under repair, commonly marked with notices simply stating 'GUR', may be any part of the course which the committee feels to be unfit for golf, such as a newly seeded area, or ground mashed up by a tractor ruts, or even patches of rough land. In that case the GUR will be clearly marked or defined in the local rules on the card. Some courses, for example, rule that gravel paths provided for golf carts are GUR. In addition, and without any special marking, material piled for removal and holes made by greenkeepers are automatically GUR. That expression 'material piled for removal' is widely cited by unscrupulous golfers seeking a free drop and there was once a scoundrel of a caddie who carried a small bag of grass clippings with him. Whenever his man had a bad lie, this caddie would surreptitiously sprinkle a handful of clippings on to the ball, and then urge his player to avail himself of the GUR loop-hole.

An element of common sense is needed in deciding whether you are entitled to free drop. The words 'piled for removal' clearly imply that there must be a definite pile. If the greenkeeper has strewn the cuttings over a wide area then obviously he has no intention of removing them. Also, if the cuttings are old, brown and rotting, then it is fair to assume that whatever the intention may have been in the first case, the material is no longer destined for removal.

CASUAL WATER

As for the casual water, the definition says that it must be visible before or after you have taken your stance. In practice if you stand by your ball and water oozes up by the welt of your golf shoe, then you can claim relief. The water must be temporary, of course, but it would include an overflow from a regular water hazard provided it was outside the defined boundary of the hazard.

Snow and ice are included in the definition but they may also be treated as loose impediments, entirely at the discretion of the golfer. One excessively devious golfer sought relief from such conditions by saying that while he was a right-hander, he wanted to play that particular shot left-handed – and in that case his stance was affected by a puddle. He wanted a free drop and the incident was put to the Rules of Golf Committee for judgement.

It was decided that the golfer was entitled to his drop, there being no restriction on ambidexterity, provided that he then actually played a left-handed shot. Do not be encouraged by that incident to try and pull a fast one. A recent rule denies relief in cases where an unnecessarily abnormal stance or swing is proposed.

By now there should be no confusion about the slight variations in procedure in hazards. If you are in casual water, GUR or burrowing animal scrape in a bunker, you drop in the bunker – or if you prefer you can drop outside the bunker for a penalty shot. If your ball is lost in such conditions in a bunker, then you drop another ball in the bunker without penalty.

PROCEDURE

Golfers are notoriously lax in the matter of free drops. A player may be scrupulously honest in determining whether his ball is in ground under repair but then, satisfied that he is entitled to relief, he takes undue advantage of what he regards as his good luck. The rules are not intended to bestow an advantage, simply to neutralise a piece of bad luck and we should be meticulous in determining the exact area where we are entitled to drop the ball. The first thing to establish is the *nearest* point which avoids the condition, and which is not nearer the hole, nor in a bunker nor on a green. Thus, in the case of casual water, there is no question of choosing which side of the puddle you prefer for your drop. That must be established as a matter of fact. It may be that the nearest point is in rough, whereas the puddle is on the fairway. Hard lines. It may be that the nearest point puts you behind a tree whereas the other side of the puddle would give you a clear shot at the green. Hard lines again. You may even decide to forego your right to a free drop and play from the puddle rather than drop into such unfavourable spots. That is your privilege. But, provided that you stoically accept these unfortunate circumstances then you may, with the clearest conscience, equally enjoy the benefits when a free drop improves your position. Having determined the *nearest* point which provides relief, you drop within one club-length of that point. When you take relief it must be complete relief. You may not, for example, drop your ball on an inviting patch of grass if it means that your foot will be in ground under repair when you take your stance.

ON THE GREEN

On the green there is an extra element of relief. Here your ball or stance do not have to be directly affected. Provided the casual water, animal scrape or GUR interferes with the line of your putt, you may place your ball on the nearest spot which gives you maximum relief, although you must never place your ball nearer the hole. The idea is to remove the source of sheer bad luck which has befallen you by a chance of nature, not to give positive help.

IMPEDIMENTS AND OBSTRUCTIONS

An area of confusion for many people is the distinction between loose impediments and obstructions, which is which, and what can you do about them. The simple rule of thumb is that impediments are objects made by nature; obstructions are objects made by man. So impediments include fallen twigs, leaves, loose stones, worm casts and rabbit dung. 'Loose' means that the object is not fixed, not growing and not adhered to the ball. Obstructions would cover such debris as discarded drink cans and cigarette packets (both of which ought to be deposited in litter baskets but are all too often just thrown down at random these days). A thoughtlessly discarded bottle once tragically may have cost the Irishman Harry Bradshaw an Open Championship, which should serve as a potent reminder to us all to curb any litter-bug tendencies. Other common examples of obstructions would be greenkeeper's equipment, or fence posts protecting plantations of young trees and hedges. So if the club captain had an air shot and collapsed with mortification on the 4th fairway, his inert body would be a loose impediment but the club which had fallen from his hand would be an obstruction. Roads and paths, with their curbs, are obstructions. Most courses contain buildings used for course-maintenance equipment, or telegraph poles or some such extraneous objects. The committee has the power to decide which, if any, of these things are to be defined as integral parts of the course. In that case the fact will be clearly stated on the card of the course and they are not obstructions. Sprinkler heads, now standard equipment on most courses, are normally classified as obstructions and if one interferes with the lie of your ball or your stance, you can drop one club-length clear without penalty.

Loose impediments (23)

The simpler of these two problems is the loose impediment. In essence, you are allowed to move any debris which qualifies as a loose impediment, with no penalty, except when both the ball and the impediment are in a hazard. So a big stone can be thrown out of the way, a broken branch can be hauled clear and fallen leaves and fir cones can be cleared.

The other important point to bear in mind is that the impediment must be loose. If, for example, your ball lay on hard-packed sand you would be entirely out of order to pick away with your finger-nail at the sand behind the ball. That would constitute illegally improving the lie. Sand and loose soil are only impediments on the green.

Obstructions (24)

The general rule with obstructions is that if you can move

the obstruction you do so and if it is too heavy or firmly fixed into the ground you move the ball, even in bunkers or on the green. No matter. Obstructions are really artifacts which are superfluous to the game of golf and therefore you are entitled to relief from them without penalty. If your ball happens to move while you are lifting an obstruction, there is no penalty (unlike in the case when moving an impediment) and you replace the ball in its original lie.

One of the hoary old stories of golf which has been handed down from generation to generation is that the way to beat a Scotsman is to wait until his ball lands in a bunker. Then you craftily throw a coin into the bunker and the Scot, by definition a thrifty creature, will not be able to stop himself from falling on the coin with cries of delight at his good fortune. Even as he slips it into his pocket you inform him that he has incurred a two stroke penalty. It is not a very funny story and has absolutely no validity in golf law since a coin, being man-made, is an obstruction and it can be removed from the hazard with impunity. So don't waste your money on that dodge.

But while obstructions normally give the golfer no cause for worry, there is one facet of the rule which does create friction. Golfers get it into their heads that they are entitled to relief from obstructions and they seem to imagine that this means complete freedom to drop in a position which gives them a completely clear shot. And there they make a big mistake. Many a card has been ruined by disqualification because of an excessively liberal view of the obstruction concession. So let us look at what the rule says with some care. If the obstruction is movable, as for instance the grass box of a lawnmower, you can move it regardless of where your ball may be. A hosepipe used for water on greens is another common example. If it interferes with the shot, move it – although in that particular example it is only proper that you put it back the way it was after you have completed the hole. But if it is immovable – say a greenkeeper's shed or an electricity pylon – and your ball lies so close to it that the obstruction interferes with your stance or restricts your intended swing, then you are entitled to a free drop. You must determine the nearest point which allows a clear swing and then measure off one club-length from that spot. So if you are behind a shed, it may still loom in front of you after you have dropped your club-length. This is just your bad luck. The rule is not intended to give you a clear shot, only to give you room to make a full swing. You have no right to a clear line of vision for your shot. You will still have to play round the shed or try a do-or-die effort to loft your ball over it. You get free relief if your ball is lost in an immovable obstruction.

The only exception to this harsh judgement is if you happen to find your ball against an obstruction so that it is behind you, interfering with your backswing. Now there is nowhere for you to drop which is not nearer the hole, and we know by now that the ball must never be dropped or allowed to roll nearer the hole. In that case you can go to the nearest side of the obstruction, determine the spot which affords a clear swing and measure off one club-length from there.

One of the rare examples in the rules of golf which demonstrates a hint of humanity within the stony hearts of the lawmakers concerns bird's nests. By the definition we have been discussing, the nests of birds full of eggs or fledgelings must be loose impediments, since they are quite clearly natural objects not fixed or growing and not adhering to the ball. Yet the rules of golf say otherwise. There is no need for vandalism if your ball lands near a bird's nest. It has been specially classified as an immovable obstruction, entirely contrary to the letter and spirit of the definition, and you may drop clear without a moment's hesitation to consider whether you would be justified in making an omelette of a clutch of plover's eggs in order to save your par.

There was one famous case of the machinations of the obstruction rule when a player in a championship hit his ball through the clubhouse window. There was no local rule defining the clubhouse as out of bounds or an integral part of the course, so the player, with admirable aplomb, strode into the smoking room, asked for a window to be opened, and played the ball back to the green. The window, in his view, was a movable obstruction. The committee gave weighty deliberations to this case and finally decided that by opening the window the player should have incurred a two stroke penalty for improving the line of his play. The window was a part of an immovable obstruction and should not have been moved. It would have been perfectly in order for the golfer to have moved a chair or table but not the window. This ruling was subsequently reversed by the Rules of Golf Committee.

Oddly enough, in a parallel case with a loose impediment, the ruling went the other way. A large branch fell from a tree and it was decided to be quite proper for a player to break off a small branch. As for the question of what is movable, that is up to you and the power of your biceps. In one competition a player's ball landed against a heavy branch which had been brought down in a storm. Since he could not move this loose impediment he declared his ball unplayable and dropped clear under penalty. Another player had the same predicament later in the day. With the help of some husky caddies he managed to drag the branch clear and it was ruled that he had been perfectly in order to do so.

OBSTRUCTION WHAMMY

A player may obtain relief from an obstruction through the green without penalty by determining the point nearest the ball which is (a) not nearer the hole, (b) avoids interference from the obstruction, and (c) is not in a hazard or on a green. However, if the ball is in a bunker the player must drop the ball in accordance with (a), (b) and (c) except that he must drop it in the bunker. So Rule 24 is quite clear and unequivocal: when taking relief from an obstruction in a bunker the ball must be dropped simultaneously both not in a hazard and also in the hazard. Whammy! Do not despair. The Rules of Golf committees in their infinite wisdom have rejected the obvious solution to this dilemma, namely to require the player to drop his ball in the bunker in accordance with (a) and (b). Instead they have provided a tortuous DECISION (24-2b/5) which leaves Rule 24 unchanged and therefore impossible to apply while at the same time insisting that the ball be dropped in the bunker. This situation raises the question of whether a Decision takes precedence over a Rule of Golf.

5 | HAZARDS

In the course of discussing the different rules of golf we have touched on most of the regulations governing hazards, if only by way of mentioning that exceptional procedures apply to hazards. So this chapter will necessarily cover much of the ground we have already covered. There is no harm in that. Repetition is one way of learning the rules and it will be helpful to retrace our steps through the bunkers of golf law and smooth out any irregularities of misconceptions and doubt.

The first thing to get absolutely clear is what the rules mean by a hazard. Golf-course architects in their infinite cunning present the golfer with all manner of obstacles. The inviting swathe of mown fairway is interrupted or bounded by features of special difficulty for the golfer to negotiate and they are not all hazards by any means. The rules define the two varieties of hazard: bunkers and water hazards. Let us start with the bunker.

Bunkers

Golfers commonly use the words 'hazard' and 'bunker' (and 'trap') as different ways of saying the same thing. The rules are more precise. Bare patches, scrapes, roads, tracks and paths are not hazards – and they are not ground under repair either, unless specifically marked. The official definition of a bunker calls it *an area of bare ground, often a depression, which is usually covered with sand*. Recalling that important provision that every word in the rules means what it says, we can now look at the definition and see that the grass-covered banks of bunkers are not part of the bunker. The rules go on to make that very point and further make it clear that islands of grass within a bunker, such as the famous church pews at Oakmont, are not part of the hazard.

The vital factor is the presence of grass. Grass surroundings, or islands of grass, or grass banks are not part of the bunker. Nor are artificial bankings, usually made of stone or wood, which are found on some courses.

Many courses have grassy depressions, in some cases legacies of wartime bomb craters which the clubs have left to grow over and remain. Sometimes they are provided by the architect as landscaping features. Others occur naturally. We golfers loosely refer to them as 'grass bunkers', an expression we now know to be a contradiction in terms. They are not hazards under the rules so if you play a wrong ball from such a 'grass bunker' you are not entitled to immunity from penalty. You must follow the standard wrong-ball procedure.

GROUNDING THE CLUB (13)

Having got that point clear, we can immediately settle one of the oldest arguments in golf. This subject produces long and noisy altercations in club bars every week, namely: What happens if a golfer touches anything with his club during the backswing of his stroke in a bunker? The rules say that before making a stroke the player shall not touch the ground in a hazard with a club or otherwise. So what happens if you brush the sand with your clubhead on the backswing? And is it the same if you touch the grass on the banking? The answer is that touching the grass (or stone or wood banking) involves no infringement since it is not part of the hazard. Touching the sand on your backswing is an offence since 'a stroke' is defined as a forward motion of the club and you have thus touched the ground before making a stroke. The general penalty applies – two shots penalty or loss of hole in match play. Let further argument cease.

For this reason it is a sound plan to play sand shots with a steep uplift of the club in order to avoid the risk of brushing the sand on the backswing. Fortunately, most teachers prescribe this method as the best technique for sand shots anyway.

FINDING THE BALL

Let us recap the rules about finding your ball in a hazard. You can brush aside enough sand or leaves or other debris to determine the presence of a golf ball. It need not necessarily be yours and you are not entitled to uncover it sufficiently to identify it as such. Do not fret; there is no penalty for playing a wrong ball provided you then go back and play the right one, and such shots with a wrong ball do not count either.

OBSTRUCTIONS AND IMPEDIMENTS

Having found your ball, or a ball, you are at liberty to remove any obstructions (artificial objects such as cigarette packets and soft-drink cans). What you must not do is touch any loose impediments (natural objects like leaves and twigs) except by the minimum amount necessary to discover a buried ball. And you must not touch the surface of the sand with your club or hand to test the surface or in any way improve the lie of your ball. Your only entitlement is to ground your feet firmly in taking your stance. That should be enough to give you all the information you need about the consistency of the lie for you to plan the type of shot to play.

You may be wondering why you can move loose impediments through the green but not when they are in, or touching, a hazard. It sounds a bit of an anomaly. Not really. The spirit of golf (which the rules seek to protect) is that hazards should be exactly that – nasty places to be avoided if possible and difficult to escape from without dropping a shot. Many professionals forget that concept. They play sand shots so well that they expect to play out of bunkers without detriment to their scores. They complain bitterly about a bad lie in a bunker having cost them a stroke. You are expected to get a bad lie in a hazard – that's why they are filled with soft sand or water. You are supposed to avoid hazards; they are deliberately sited to punish a bad shot. No sympathy is called for in the case of a bad lie in a hazard and complaints about the rough conditions in hazards should be ignored. Oakmont, the famous American championship course, has a machine specially designed to plough furrows in bunkers and guarantee a positively bad lie every time.

Similar strictures apply to the design of pot bunkers just big enough and deep enough, in the immortal phrase of the late Bernard Darwin, 'to hold an angry man and his mashie'. If you get into one of these fairway pot bunkers at St Andrews, you might as well abandon all hope of getting on to the green; often enough you will be doing well to get back on to the fairway with your recovery stroke. If you elect to declare your ball unplayable in a bunker, you can play it from the place where it was last played.

CASUAL WATER, BALL LOST OR UNPLAYABLE

We can now look briefly once more at the other rules governing hazards. In a bunker, if your ball lies in casual water, ground under repair or casts made by burrowing animals, or if these conditions interfere with your stance or the area of your intended swing, you may take relief in the normal way by dropping a ball in the bunker, without penalty, on a spot which gives maximum relief from these conditions. Or you can drop a ball outside the bunker for one penalty stroke. If your ball is lost in such conditions in a hazard – and you must have good reasons for believing it to be lost – you may drop another ball in the hazard in the same manner, again without penalty. You can declare your ball unplayable in a bunker but in that case you may not invoke the full range of unplayable-ball options. You can only drop a ball in the bunker under penalty of one stroke or adopt the stroke-and-distance procedure.

SMOOTHING THE SAND

Hazards impose special obligations on golfers under the etiquette of the game. The player whose ball goes into a bunker is often an angry man, and when we lose our tempers we often lose our good manners as well. It is no less than common courtesy to smooth out your footprints after playing out of bunkers and on that subject a short digression is in order, in the form of a plea to tournament players.

All of us are conditioned in our golfing behaviour to some degree by what we see on television, or in person, of the great players. We copy their mannerisms – the bad ones as well as the good all too often – while trying to copy their swings. The process may be subconscious but it is a fact and it puts a responsibility on the stars which they are not always quick to acknowledge or accept.

Slow play, the bane of golf, obviously derives to a large extent from this process of aping the great players, particularly their tedious dithering over putts. In the present context of bunker play, how often do you see a tournament professional play out of a bunker beside the green and then clamber up the face, using his wedge like a climbing pick and imprinting deep footmarks in the sand? He knows that there is an employee standing by – but probably out of shot – with a rake to restore the bunker to its pristine condition. But the TV viewer will retain that image of the mountaineering golfer leaving the bunker looking like a battlefield and he may do the same thing in his own golf – when there is no rake man there to tidy up after him. How much more thoughtful it would be if the professionals made a point of always smoothing their footprints (if only in token gestures) and retracing their steps in the prescribed manner out of the back of the bunker. Then we would all subconsciously get the message of the correct form.

The rules do not oblige you to smooth your footprints after playing your shot; they simply say that there is no penalty if you do so, provided you do nothing to improve the lie of your ball or help your subsequent play of the hole.

That rule had to be scrutinised with some care by officials at the 1969 US Masters when Arnold Palmer played a shot in a bunker, failed to get out and then angrily swung his club again, splashing it into the sand in a 'replay' of his original stroke. A referee penalised him two strokes for grounding his club in a bunker. Palmer was not happy with that ruling and sought advice from an official of the United States Golf Association. A committee meeting was hurriedly called and before the round was completed Palmer was told that the penalty had been rescinded. That decision caused a fine old controversy. Clearly the committee had been guided by the spirit of the rules which are designed to prevent the player from improving his lie or helping him in his play. But many people felt that the referee had been quite right in imposing the penalty, particularly in view of a decision by the Rules of Golf Committee in a similar case. That decision reads, in part: 'Rule 33-1 is mandatory in that when a player is about to play out of a bunker he is not permitted to touch the ground in a hazard before making his stroke. After making a stroke in a hazard he must ensure that he is not required immediately to play another stroke from that hazard before he touches the ground with his club.' Palmer got the benefit of the considerable doubt in that case and the best advice is never to replay a stroke in a bunker, in hot or cold blood.

A rather different incident was put to the Rules of Golf Committee when a player accidentally dropped his club in the sand before playing. Here justice prevailed with the ruling that no penalty was due. Another famous incident was the action of Tom Weiskopf in the last round of a tournament which he happened to be leading. In that tense situation he wanted to be absolutely certain of his yardages for a critical approach shot. He therefore marched purposefully forward making a bee-line for the flag and his path took him straight through the middle of a greenside bunker. Having completed his yardage count, Weiskopf retraced his steps and on the way back he meticulously smoothed away his footprints in the bunker. The question now arose: had he improved his line for his subsequent play of the hole? It was ruled that he had not. At most he had restored the line to its original condition, although the officials might have found this decision more difficult if Weiskopf had then played into that bunker. They might have then felt justified in ruling that the surface had been tested before making the stroke. In the actual event, they had no great problem in exonerating Weiskopf, although some people felt at the time that a general penalty might have been warranted on the grounds of unduly delaying play.

Water Hazards

A water hazard is officially any sea, lake, pond, river, ditch, surface drainage ditch or other open water course, regardless of whether or not it contains water. Any island of land is part of the hazard. Now while the banks of a bunker are not part of the hazard, the same is clearly not true of a water hazard. The water level of a pond may have fallen, or dried up completely, leaving a grassy bank and that most definitely *is* in the hazard. It is the duty of the committee to define clearly the limits of water hazards and this is usually done by means of coloured stakes or lines.

LATERAL WATER HAZARDS

A lateral water hazard fulfils all the above conditions. It lies more or less in the direction of the line of play, thus making it impracticable to drop a ball behind it. Once again it is up to the committee to define the lateral water hazards in a clear and distinctive manner because a slightly different procedure has to be used with them.

WATER-HAZARD RULES

Now water hazards. If your ball goes into a hazard, you are at liberty to play it as it lies, of course. This is an option which many golfers never consider, although professionals often take off their shoes and socks and wade into the water to play wonderful recoveries. Lu Liang Huan, the Formosan who came so close to winning the British Open at Royal Birkdale in 1971, played a masterly stroke from water several inches deep in the last round of the Moroccan Grand Prix of 1974. Unfortunately, as at Birkdale, he came second on that occasion, so we cannot describe his aquatic shot as a winner.

The Barcelona Golf Club, El Prat, has a water hazard which is designed to tempt the player to have a go. The water is kept at a depth of just over an inch, so it is a fair gamble for the golfer to chance his arm and risk soaking himself in the club-head's bow-wave. Wet or dry, you must not ground your club in a water hazard. (If the ball is in muddy water you can rake about with a club to find it and there is no penalty if you move the ball, provided you either replace it or take lawful relief under penalty.)

Perhaps you do not care to risk it. Well, if your ball is in a water hazard – and it need not be in actual water, as we have seen – you may drop a ball either under stroke and distance or anywhere behind the hazard on a line keeping the point where your ball last crossed the margin of the hazard between you and the hole. You have to pay a one shot penalty, of course, and you adopt the identical procedure if your ball is lost in the water hazard. As we have seen earlier you must drop the ball on that line, not at arm's length to either side.

Obviously you may not be able to drop a ball behind a lateral water hazard because, by definition, the direction of the lateral water hazard may make that impossible. So, provided that the hazard is clearly defined as a 'lateral', you may drop under penalty under the normal water-hazard rules or, in addition, within two club-lengths on either side of the hazard opposite the point at which your ball went in.

Examples

The best way to learn a rule is through the hard example of personal experience. It can take years to acquire your knowledge that way, and the purpose of this book is to short-circuit that painful process. So the next best thing is to provide some examples so that you can identify with the players and benefit from their experiences at second hand.

The examples which follow are all based on decisions which have been handed down on appeal by the Rules of Golf committees. Let us start with an incident which probably sounded hilarious to the player's friends when they heard about it, but which was clearly no joke to the player at the time. His ball lay in a water hazard, on a bank, and he decided to play it. Alas, he hit it out of bounds. Now, under the stroke-and-distance rule, he had to drop on to that bank. You can guess what happened – the ball rolled down the bank (less than two club-lengths) into the water.

The question – and how we can sympathise with the agonised player – was whether he had to take two spoonfuls of penalty medicine or whether, in the name of Christian charity and simple justice and the principles of double jeopardy, he might just this once be allowed to place his ball on the bank? In these multiple-disaster cases, it is important to keep a cool head and follow the horrendous sequence step by step, applying the appropriate rules as we go along. Having hit a ball out of bounds the player had no option but to follow the stroke-and-distance course. That is past history by the time he came to drop on the bank and cannot influence anything which might happen. The fact of having just gone out of bounds is irrelevant to the dropping situation. So when his ball rolled down into the water, he had no recourse but to bite on the bullet and pay another penalty to retrieve it under the water-hazard rules.

Two balls are in a bunker and while the first player is taking his shot, the other player stands in the bunker well away from his ball and leans on his club. Is he guilty of grounding his club? Yes, of course he is. That was too easy. Right. Take the same situation. Instead of leaning on his club, this time the second player takes a firm stance, still well away from his ball, and simulates the shot he is going to play but without using a club. Is he guilty of any offence? Indeed he is, said the committee. By taking what we might call a practice stance, he was unlawfully testing the condition of the surface.

In a foursome match, a player failed to get out of a bunker with his recovery shot. Now it was his partner's turn to play a bunker shot. But before leaving the bunker, the first player smoothed out his footprints. The opposition claimed the hole on the grounds that the partnership had grounded a club before playing the second bunker shot. Not at all, answered the adjudicators. Provided the lie of the ball was not improved, there was no penalty.

Try this one. In a four-ball match a divot from one player's shot landed on top of his partner's ball, which lay in a bunker. The first player removed his divot and replaced it, as all golfers should do on (nearly) every occasion. Was the first player at fault in removing his divot (loose impediment) from the bunker? And was his partner guilty of any offence? Yes, they were both guilty, replied the committee with, one cannot help feeling, some relish. The first player was due a penalty for removing a loose impediment from the bunker. His partner was equally to blame under the rule that if a player breaks a rule which might help his partner's play, the partner incurs the relative penalty as well. Thus with an elegant left and right, the Rules of Golf Committee killed two birds with one divot. However, said the committee, having had its malicious fun, in stroke-play it would have ruled differently. Then the second player would have the right to move the divot off his ball under the principle that a player is normally entitled to the lie that his shot gave him, and to relief from the results of actions by fellow competitors and outside agencies. By the same token, an *opponent's* divot could have been removed in match-play. Subsequently the Rules of Golf Committee reversed its decision and now all such divots may be removed to restore to the player the lie that his shot had given him.

A player 'thinned' his bunker shot and the ball shot over the green in that sickening way which every golfer knows all too well. He then replayed the shot twice, taking plenty of sand the way he should have done the first time. Now, however, it was discovered that his ball had gone out of bounds and he had to drop under stroke and distance in that bunker. Had he tested the surface with those practice swings? Yes, he had, ruled the committee. It was the player's responsibility to ensure that he was not going to have to play his next shot from the bunker before he took those practice swings.

A player whose ball lay in a hazard made two deliberate practice swings, digging out a liberal helping of sand each time. 'That is only two penalty strokes,' he said. 'It does not matter how many practice strokes I took, I broke only one rule.' His marker thought that four penalty strokes were due. So, in the fullness of time, did the Rules of Golf Committee. If a player *inadvertently* breaks a rule more than once in the same incident, it is usual to let him off with the penalty for a single offence. For deliberately committing two separate offences, this player should be clobbered with the full sentence of four penalty strokes.

The one clear intention of the Rules of Golf is to provide ways of completing the round no matter how seriously impeded the player may find himself. So, exceptionally, provision has been made for the nightmarish situation where a player has made a shot within a water hazard and left the ball in the hazard in a worse and unplayable lie. The normal stroke-and-distance rule would merely put him back in that first difficult lie in the hazard, with the prospect of spending the rest of the day forlornly hacking from puddle to puddle. In that case the player may, under penalty of a stroke, drop the ball on the spot from which his last stroke *outside the hazard* was played.

On that happy note, let us be done with hazards, smooth out our footprints and move on to the next phase of the game.

WATER-HAZARD WHAMMY

By now we understand that when a ball goes into a water hazard, or a lateral water hazard, we don't bother watching for the splash because the ultimate watery destination of the ball is irrelevant; the important point of reference is the exact spot where the ball last crossed the margin of the hazard. Establish that spot and everything flows from there. Or does it? There is one circumstance in which the rule is stood on its head. If you hit a ball into a river or stream and the current carries it out of bounds you must (Decision 26-1/7) follow the out of bounds procedure, ie stroke and distance. Whammy! That Decision seems to be seriously at odds with the main body of golf law. A water hazard is officially defined as any sea, lake, pond, river, ditch, surface drainage ditch or other water course and the Definition adds that all water within the margin of a water hazard is part of the water hazard. So when Pebble Beach golf club defines the Pacific Ocean as a lateral water hazard all the water within the margin of the Pacific Ocean is part of the hazard. So even if a water course carries your ball into the ocean, even unto the shores of Australia, it is still in the hazard and NOT out of bounds.

6 | ON THE GREEN

Putting is often called 'a game within a game' and the expression is doubly apt. It is true in the physical sense that after the *Donner und Blitzen* of golf through the green, straining every muscle to pour power into majestic drives and towering iron shots, the golfer must now change character and adopt the delicate approach of a watchmaker, bringing all his command of eye and touch and feeling into play with subtlety and fine precision. This contrast, more pronounced than in any other game, gives golf its unique distinction and charm as well, some might think, as its chief source of frustration. What changes we might have seen in the roll of the great champions if putting had not been of such paramount importance to the score.

Putting is also a game within a game in golf law. There are some significant departures from usual golfing principles as soon as your ball reaches the green and that, incidentally, means when any part of your ball touches the prepared putting surface.

PITCH MARKS (16)

You are now ready to putt and before you do so there are a number of things you can do to improve your chances of success. You can repair pitch marks made by the impact of balls landing on the green. As a matter of good golfing manners, you should always repair your own pitch mark and if you get a chance to repair such craters left by golfers less thoughtful than yourself, then by all means do so, provided you do not dally on the green and unduly hold up play.

Make absolutely certain that the damage you are repairing is a pitch mark. The bane of modern golf with watered greens and deep cleats on golf shoes is the proliferation of spike marks in the form of raised tuffets or scratches which can deflect the ball. These must not be repaired and you should take care not to flatten them either by walking along the line of your putt or in the course of repairing a pitch mark. One often sees golfers mend a pitch mark by jabbing at it with a tee peg or repair tool and then flattening the area by pressing down on it with a foot. That practice is not illegal in itself but the act of standing on the pitch mark may incidentally flatten a spike mark. It is much better to get into the safe and sound golfing habit of repairing pitch marks by gently raising the depressed area with a tee peg or repair fork and then lightly flattening the surface with the sole of your putter. Do not tamp it down hard; just allow the natural weight of the putter to smooth out the irregularities. You may also repair old holes.

IMPEDIMENTS

You are also allowed to remove loose impediments from the line of your putt. These may include fallen leaves, worm-casts, sand thrown on to the green from a bunker, loose earth, snow and ice. Once again you must take great care in how you proceed in moving impediments. There is a general prohibition against improving your line as well as a specific ban on testing the surface of the green. Wholesale sweeping operations along the line of your putt would thus constitute a double infringement. One reason why golfers would like to test the surface is to discover the direction of the grain, or nap. Grass seldom grows straight upwards like the bristles on a hair brush but tends to grow in one direction. This grain is particularly pronounced on inclined courses which are in the hotter latitudes and while the rule of thumb has it that the grass grows towards the direction of the setting sun, it often happens that one green will have areas of grain in quite contrary directions.

The influence of grain on the roll of a ball can be uncannily powerful and it is common in places such as South Africa and the southern USA to watch your putt apparently defy the laws of gravity and veer *up* what is patently a *down*slope. So you need to know how the grain lies but you must not test the surface. The answer is to use your eyes. When the grain lies away from you, the grass has a glossy sheen while it appears dull or matt when the grain is towards you. Some tournament professionals actually map the grain for every green during their practice rounds in case the competition days should happen to be overcast, when 'reading the nap' becomes more difficult. So be wary about the way you brush aside loose impediments and save yourself the risk of an accusation of testing the surface. A light sweeping motion with the back of the hand or putter is recommended.

TOUCHING THE LINE

Another preliminary to putting to which you are entitled is the advice of your partner or caddie on the correct line, if only to confirm your own judgement. Former Open Champion Max Faulkner had a caddie who used to lie flat on his stomach to study the line of a putt through a pair of opera glasses from which the lenses had long since vanished and then invariably produced the advice: 'Hit it slightly straight, sir.' If you do take advice, make sure that your caddie or partner does not touch the surface of the green (16). That is illegal so the rule is 'Point, don't touch' or, better still, an oral suggestion such as 'Two inches outside the right lip.'

FLAGSTICKS (17)

You are now ready to putt and you have to decide what you would like to have done with the flagstick: taken out, attended, or left. It is a two shot penalty or loss of hole if your putt (from the green, of course) hits the flagstick, so if you decide to have it attended, be sure that the person on the flagstick knows that it must be removed before your ball reaches the hole. This is one of the commonest sources of mishap since the flagstick may jam in the hole and resist all the tugging of the attendant. When you are attending the flagstick for someone else, take the precaution of easing it so that it will come out smoothly, and if it is a windy day it is a usual courtesy to gather the folds of the actual flag in your hand, so that its flapping will not distract the person putting. On sunny days make sure you stand so that your shadow does not fall across the hole on the line of the putt.

Advocates of simplified golf rules find much ammunition in the complexities of the regulations covering the flagstick. Many of the rules do seem entirely superfluous to the essence of golf and merely achieve the highly undesirable effect of slowing the already tedious process of putting even further. However, the rules exist and must be observed, so let us quickly run through the fine print. As we have seen, you may elect, before making your stroke, to have the flagstick left as it is, attended, removed or held up. If you have been unwise enough to leave the flagstick in the hole, once your ball has been struck you cannot shout 'Take it out!' On the green we all tend to become slightly preoccupied by the task in hand and often an opponent, or fellow competitor, or caddie, will automatically attend the flag. If this is done with your knowledge, and you make no objection, then you are assumed to have authorised it. However, if it is done *without* your knowledge or authority, and you should then hit the flagstick or the attendant with your ball, there is no penalty. You play the ball as it lies. Finally, there are the occasions when you play from off the green and your ball lodges agonisingly against the flagstick, suspended above the hole but without dropping. Now you may have the flagstick removed – best to do the job yourself, with great care – and if the ball drops then you have holed out with your last shot.

CROQUET PUTTING (16)

In making your actual stroke, remember that croquet putting has been banned. That is, you must not stand astride a line extending from the hole through your ball. Many golfers were dismayed when croquet putting was outlawed because the method certainly enabled them to make a decent stroke after their nerves had long since rendered orthodox putting ineffective. On balance, however, croquet putting was foreign to the traditions of golf and while the ban may have been hard on certain individuals, it did at least preserve golfing orthodoxy. If you find that putting is much easier when you have two eyes facing directly at the hole, then try the style adopted by Sam Snead. He faces the hole and putts with the ball alongside his right foot, steadying the top of his putter with the left hand and swinging the club with a pushing movement of his right hand held down the shaft.

BALL OVERHANGING HOLE (16)

It often happens that your putt will run right to the lip of the hole and then stop, greatly to your chagrin. In that case, the rules allow you to wait only ten seconds for the putt to drop. You must not dance around the hole, or blow at the ball in your frustration (as once happened in a competition) or stand like a statue in the hope that the ball will finally topple over the brink. What you should do is walk to the hole and then let your conscience count off ten seconds. You gain no advantage by waiting longer than ten seconds because if the ball drops after the time limit has expired you are deemed to have holed out with your previous stroke and you incur a penalty stroke. If you wait more than ten seconds and the ball does not drop there is no penalty, provided that you do not unduly delay play.

Your responsibilities on the green do not end when you hole out. You have an obligation to show due courtesy to others while they putt. That means standing still, well out of their area of vision, and keeping quiet.

MARKING THE BALL (16)

Now for the troublesome business of when to mark your ball and what happens if your ball accidentally hits someone else's. The normal rule of golf applies that the ball furthest from the hole is to be played first and in stroke-play if there is another competitor's ball remotely near the line of your putt you may ask him to mark and lift it. In practice, most players usually mark and lift their balls automatically, in order to clean them, and only replace them when it is their turn to putt. If you fail to take these elementary precautions, which ought to become a matter of habit, and your ball hits a fellow competitor's, then you incur a two stroke penalty. The other player's ball must immediately be replaced in its original position.

Anyone – player, fellow competitor or opponent may mark and lift his ball at his own discretion or require any other ball to be marked and lifted. This reform should end all penalties for striking another ball and all discussions about which ball has to be replaced because in practice everyone except the player about to putt will have safely removed his ball.

The marking of the ball is one of the favourite areas for that tiny minority of rogues who are looking for illegal advantage and there was one professional who was notorious for his sly attempts to cheat. He was finally cured of his unorthodox sleight of hand with a ball marker during the British Professional Match-play Championship when his opponent announced curtly: 'Mark your ball again and I'll give you the putt'. It was in order to eliminate that kind of behaviour, or even the suspicion of it, that the Rules now include instructions for the proper marking of a ball on the green. Using a small coin, or a regular ball-marker specially made for the purpose, you should place is as close to the ball as possible, pressing it firmly into the turf at the point furthest from the hole. In other words, you line up the hole, ball and marker and when you come to replace the ball by its marker it will be returned to its original position with no possibility of having gained an iota of advantage. (One common method of cheating is to mark the ball with the marker between ball and hole and then to replace the ball in front of the marker, thus 'stealing' a fractional, if helpful, advantage.) It may be that your opponent or fellow competitor asks you to move your marker to one side as it might interfere with the roll of his putt. In that case you proceed as above, marking and lifting the ball, and then measure off a club-head's width (or two, as requested) to the side, as near as possible to a right-angle to the line between your marker and the hole. When you replace the ball you first measure back the width of a club-head, move the marker, put down the ball and then lift the marker. If you cannot trust yourself accurately to judge a right-angle when moving the marker to one side, you can easily take a fix on some land-mark such as a tree or fence post to fix the positions. What you do not do in these cases is to measure off one club-head's width from the ball itself and then mark the other end of the putter head. That way is sloppy and open to abuse. By the same token, it is bad form to mark your ball by planting a tee-peg alongside it, since you may raise a spike mark in removing the peg, and it is no less than petty vandalism to mark the ball by scoring the turf with the point of a tee peg. Anywhere on the course a ball to be lifted must first be marked.

CONCESSIONS

In match-play, if you wish to concede your opponent a putt without requiring him to hole out, there are two points to be borne in mind. Firstly, it is essential to make the concession in absolutely unambiguous terms. If he putts up close and you say 'That's good' it could be taken as a compliment on his skill or as an expression of conceding the next putt.

Strictly speaking, you should remove his ball and hand it to him as a formal act of concession, but that is not always convenient if you are standing yards away waiting to make your putt. So, if you concede verbally, say so in unequivocal terms and then there can be no confusion.

The other point about these concessions is to eliminate all feeling of guilt. The man who bridles because he has not been conceded a 12in putt is halfway to being beaten, especially if he allows his resentment to simmer on until the next tee. He will surely hit a bad drive because an angry golfer is a bad golfer. It is a sound idea to discipline yourself never to anticipate a concession and, consequently, never to feel disappointment when it does not come. Eliminate all thoughts of so-called sportsmanship in this area. There is nothing unsporting about wanting to see a short putt holed out and so if you putt up close to the hole, go straight to your ball and mark it. That way, you will be mentally preparing yourself for the short one and will be more likely to hole it if necessary. If you never expect a concession you will never lose your mental equilibrium. You may concede your opponent's next stroke, the hole or the match and that concession may not be declined or withdrawn.

BALL ON THE WRONG GREEN

On occasions your ball will land on a green other than the one to which you were playing. By now you will have realised that the spirit and customs of golf are opposed to golfers digging divots out of pristine putting surfaces with deep-soled pitching wedges. The rules of golf have anticipated your dilemma. In this event you must lift your ball and drop it without penalty off the green, as near as possible to where it lay but not nearer the hole and not into a hazard.

CASUAL WATER

As for the other eventualities which may arise on the green, the commonest is casual water (including snow and ice) but you can also meet examples of ground under repair (properly marked) and holes and scrapes made by burrowing animals. In this instance the condition does not have to affect the lie of the ball or your stance but may be anywhere on a line between your ball – provided it is on the green – and the hole. If so, you may lift your ball without penalty and *place* it in the nearest position which provides maximum relief. If your ball is off the green you get no relief from such conditions intervening on the green. The reason for stressing that word 'place' is to underline the fact that a ball is never dropped on a green. If you have lawful occasion to lift and move your ball, you may tee it up if on a teeing ground, you must drop it through the green – and that includes fairways, rough and hazards – and you must place it on the green.

When greenkeepers cut a new hole they use the plug of turf to fill in the old hole. These plugs sometimes sink, or shrink in hot weather, and create a problem for the golfer. Treat them in the same way as pitch marks and repair them as best you can. If your efforts at restoring the surface are unsuccessful, as they might well be if the plug was badly shrivelled, then you must request the committee to repair the blemish or give you permission to move your ball to give yourself a clear line to the hole.

RELIEF WHAMMY

It is always easier to remember a rule if it is based on logic. Take the example of relief from abnormal ground conditions. If the ball is on the green common sense tells us that the ball must be placed because dropping might damage the putting surface. Common sense also tells us that the ball must be dropped through the green because that is the standard method of putting a ball into play. And if a ball is put into play on the teeing ground you are at liberty to put it on a tee peg because that is a universal right. Ninety-nine times out of a hundred you will do the right thing by following common sense. But wait. If your ball is sitting in a puddle on the green and the nearest point of relief is on the fairway then logic will betray you because for some inscrutable reason known only to the golf legislators you now have to PLACE the ball. And does the reverse apply? If your ball is in a puddle on the fairway and the nearest point of relief is on the green do you now DROP the ball on the green? No. You have to determine the nearest point which is not in a hazard or on a green and measure off your club-length from there. Then drop. Whammy!

7 RIGHTS AND DUTIES

MARKING THE CARD (6)

In April 1968 an estimated twenty million people watching the live telecast of the climax of the US Masters saw Roberto de Vincenzo get down in three strokes on the 17th hole. That birdie was enough to put the popular Argentinian in a tie with Bob Goalby. There would have to be a play-off in the morning to settle the issue. Roberto walked off the last green to a standing ovation which was as much a tribute to his outstanding sportmanship and skill over his distinguished career as to his play in this final round. At the age of 45, Roberto was running out of time if he was to add the green jacket of the Masters champion to his British Open Championship medal. No man, save possibly Sam Snead, had won more tournaments (neither had a clear idea of how many victories they had achieved) but the classics had largely escaped Roberto. Here was his chance and it was a moment of high emotion as he signed his card and handed it to the recorder. Then came the bombshell. It was announced that Roberto had signed an incorrect card. The total was correct but the figures did not tally because the marker, Tommy Aaron, had inadvertently entered a 4 opposite the 17th hole. The rule admitted no possibility of a loop-hole; it stated unequivocally that if a player signed for a score lower than his actual score he must be disqualified. And if he signed for a higher score than his actual score (as in this case) then that score must stand. It did not make any difference that eyewitnesses by the thousand were prepared to swear to that birdie. (Actually, their testimony would not have been conclusive since it is possible that if, say, Roberto's ball had moved at the address, only he and his marker would have known about it.) Nor could there be any special dispensation under the rule of equity; the rules did not admit that possibility. It was quite clear that the spurious 4 would have to stand, as attested by the signatures of player and marker.

There were plenty of precedents, including the equally tragic case of Mrs Jackie Pung, whose cup of triumph in the 1957 US Women's Open was dashed from her lips in identical fashion. So the green blazer was ceremoniously presented to Bob Goalby. It proved to be a hollow victory. Instead of winning the universal plaudits which he had legitimately earned, he was widely regarded as the man who took the Masters by default. That feeling, totally unfair to Goalby, who was bitterly disappointed that he could not play off with Roberto for an unambiguous decision, cost him thousands of dollars from commercial endorsements. We can never say that the mistake by the marker cost Roberto the Masters – and for two reasons. Firstly, and obviously, no one can assert what the outcome of the play-off might have been. Secondly, and more importantly, the responsibility for returning an accurate card rests squarely on the player.

The marker's job is to check the score with the competitor for each hole and record it. But the competitor himself is solely responsible for the correctness of the card which he signs. No alterations can be made to a card after it has been signed and handed in to the committee. As a matter of incidental interest, the Roberto de Vicenzo affair persuaded the Masters committee to institute the procedure of having competitors go to a special tent behind the 18th green where they can sit quietly, compose their emotions and calmly check their cards before signing them. Any doubtful points can be cleared up at this time.

What exactly is the information which a competitor is required to provide on his card before he adds his signature? Well, in club events, which is the highest form of competitive golf to which most of us aspire, the player has a duty before starting play to see that the card issued to him by the committee has marked on it his name and his current handicap. Make sure those details are correct before you hit a ball because if you play off a higher handicap than your current one, you will be disqualified. And if you play off a lower handicap than your correct one then the score stands off that lower handicap. As for the other entries on the card, the rules make only one requirement – that the gross score for each hole shall be entered in the appropriate spaces. You are not required to work out your nett scores, nor add up the totals or points. That is up to the committeemen and if you try to do their job for them you risk making a mistake which cannot be rectified later. Every year in professional tournaments some poor golfer comes to grief through entering totals. What usually happens is that the marker inadvertently enters the total for the first nine holes in the space for the ninth hole. The total is correct enough and that is what the player confirms when he signs his card. But now the committee sees a figure of 36 entered for the ninth hole. And, as we have seen, that is the score which the rules insist must be accepted. So instead of a 72, the player finds himself credited with 104 and he is out of the tournament. So always double-check the scores for individual holes; it does not matter if you make an error in the adding-up or handicap conversions. Do not sign your card and leave your marker to hand it in to the committee. There have been cases of markers forgetting to hand in cards until it was too late. It is the player's duty to hand in his own card, signed and countersigned, as soon as possible after completion of his round.

KNOW AND USE THE RULES (6)

Another important responsibility which the rules place on every competitor is that he should make himself familiar with the rules and conditions of the competition. You should also have with you copies of the rules and local rules. That may sound so fundamental as to be unnecessary but it is surprising how many golfers enter a competition with only the haziest ideas of what it is all about. You hear them on the first tee asking which tee-markers they should be using or whether winter rules are in force. Committees have wide powers to bring in local rules to cover abnormal conditions (such as excessive mud), the preservation of the course (which could mean a ban on playing off ground under repair in a recently seeded area) and allowing special relief from roads, paths or drainage trenches. In addition, the committee has a duty to provide clear definitions of water hazards, ground under repair, out of bounds, obstructions and integral parts of the course. You should take a close look at the local and competition rules before starting and it is as well to get into the habit, after putting out on each green, to consult the local rules for any special conditions governing the next hole. The strategy of your play may very well be influenced by prior knowledge of unsuspected out of bounds, or suchlike. That information should be printed on the card. Temporary local rules are usually displayed only on the club notice board. If winter rules are in force, pay particular attention to the details as such rules are liable to vary from course to course. On some occasions you may be permitted to lift, clean and place within 6in of your original lie on the fairway, not nearer the hole, and at other times the rule might be to 'roll' the ball within a club's length, not nearer the hole.

There is an idea abroad among many golfers that 'rough' must be regarded as a 'hazard' in applying the rules. In other words, if you have a free drop in a bunker, you must always drop within the bunker (25), so if in rough, you must always drop in the rough.

That is not the case at all. If your ball is in, say, casual water in the edge of the rough it may well be that you can legitimately drop out on the fairway. That is your good luck and you should take it.

On the other hand, there will be the occasions when you will have to drop from the fairway into the rough and you must accept those bad rubs of the green along with the good.

THE GOLFER'S RIGHTS

By this stage it is hoped that you have absorbed a solid grounding in the main rules of golf but that does not mean that you will never have to consult the official rule book. You certainly will, and a copy of the rules should be a permanent accessory in your golf bag. (Keep the booklet in a plastic bag so that it does not get soggy in rainy weather.) There are one or two useful hints on how to consult the book.

The first thing to do is to think in the precise, legal terms which the rules employ. That is to say, of a 'flagstick' and not 'pin' or 'stick'; 'bunker', not 'trap'; 'stroke-play', not 'medal-golf'. Distinguish clearly between the rules of match-play and stroke-play. You will find the appropriate rule from the comprehensive index and before forming a decision scrutinise the definitions to confirm that the rule applies to your exact situation. In complex cases, where more than one rule may be involved, take the sequence step by step. Distinguish between a 'ball in play', a 'provisional ball', a 'second ball' and 'ball out of play'. At any time during the round your ball may be any of these and even an outside agency. Take the example of a player in stroke-play who tees up outside the teeing ground and then drives out of bounds. Is he penalised for both infringements? The answer is, no. A ball played from outside the teeing ground is not 'in play' and therefore the fact that it goes out of bounds is irrelevant. The only penalty is for playing from outside the teeing ground.

Sometimes the sheer complexity of the incident will defy all attempts to extract an acceptable decision from the rules. Always remember that in stroke-play you have the option of playing a second ball and then letting the committee unscramble the legal niceties later. Be sure to raise the query before you sign the card. In match-play you and your opponent have to come to an agreement before moving on to the next hole. In most cases, when the natural justice of the situation suggests, you can shelve the problem by mutually agreeing on a half.

Your attitude to the rules is all important. Accept your due penalties with good grace. Fretting about your bad luck will only make matters worse because it will distract your concentration for subsequent shots. But remember that the rules can also help you on many occasions and it may be helpful to review some of the elements in what might be called the golfer's Bill of Rights.

There are many more rights which could be distilled from the rules, but this list will possibly serve to demonstrate that the laws can and should be used in a positive way and need not be seen purely as a catechism of prohibitions and penalties.

AMATEUR STATUS

The government of golf is shared between the Royal and Ancient Golf Club of St Andrews, Scotland, and the United States Golf Association. These two bodies maintain a close liaison and meet formally from time to time to consider revisions in the rules. All national associations are affiliated to one or other of the two parent organisations and are consulted before changes are introduced. In theory the government of golf may appear to be autocratic but the way it works in practice, with extensive interchange of views on an unofficial basis among all the golfing nations, is democratic enough. Proof of that assertion is to be found in the

YOU HAVE THE RIGHT TO...

- **R**e-tee your ball whenever you have reason to return to the teeing ground to play another ball (11).
- **R**e-tee your ball if it falls off the peg before you make your stroke (11).
- **R**ecall an opponent's shot played from outside the teeing ground (11).
- **R**ecall an opponent's shot played out of turn from the teeing ground (10).
- **A** free drop from ground under repair (including piled grass cuttings), scrapes made by burrowing animals and casual water (25).
- **R**emove loose impediments, except in a hazard (23).
- **R**emove movable obstructions anywhere, and to replace your ball without penalty if it moves during the removal of an obstruction (24).
- **A** free drop from immovable obstructions except in water hazards (24).
- **A**scertain from your opponent the number of strokes he has taken at any time (9).
- **R**eplace a ball which becomes unfit for play (5).
- **A**nother drop, without penalty, if you accidentally drop in a wrong place (20).
- **A**sk anyone for information about matters of fact such as distances, the line of play through the green, or about the position of the flagstick (8).
- **M**ake practice swings at any time and to play practice strokes (except in hazards) between the play of two holes, provided you do not play on or to any green except the one just played (7).
- **R**eplace any club which becomes unfit in normal play and to bring your total complement up to fourteen clubs (4).
- **I**n stroke-play to put a second ball into play in doubtful situations (3).
- **T**he lie which your shot gave you (13).
- **L**ift your ball to identify it (12).
- **S**earch for five minutes for a lost ball (27).
- **R**efrain from grounding your club in precarious rough or on the green in windy conditions, so that if your ball moves after you have taken your stance you are not penalised (18).
- **C**lean your ball before every stroke on the green (16).
- **M**ark and lift your ball on the green at any time (16).
- **R**epair pitch marks on the green (16).
- **R**eplace your ball if it is moved by an outside agency (18)
- **C**lean your ball when taking relief under the rules (21).
- **S**uspend play if you feel threatened by lightning or fall ill (6).
- **T**ake equitable evasive action for relief from physical danger (3).
- **S**eek and accept advice from your partner or either of your caddies (8).
- **A** free drop in a hazard if your ball is lost in casual water, scrapes made by burrowing animals or ground under repair in that bunker (13).
- **T**ouch grass or banking materials on your backswing when playing from a bunker (definitions).

undoubted fact that golf passes the ultimate test of democracy, in that its government is conducted by the tacit consent of the vast majority of golfers.

By and large the rules of the R and A conform exactly with those of the USGA. One major exception has been the size of the ball not less than 1.68in in diameter in countries under USGA jurisdiction and not less than 1.62in in diameter in the R and A code. Thus the bigger ball has been perfectly legal all over the world but the smaller ball was not permitted in competition in areas where the USGA writ was in force. The small ball was gradually phased out and decreed to be illegal from January 1st, 1990.

Another area of divergence is the matter of amateur status. The value of a prize which an amateur may receive without jeopardising his amateur status varies slightly, although the difference is more apparent than real. We golfers are expected, even obliged, to ensure that we do not accept a prize whose retail value exceeds the limit of $500 or £300, according to where the competition is held. In fact, that is an intolerable responsibility. What prize-winner would have the gall, or the knowledge, to challenge the value of his prize and reject it? Nobody. We have to take on trust that a competition run according to the rules of golf is conforming to the legal limits on prizes.

In general the rules of amateur status have been framed to prevent the very best amateur players from exploiting their skill and fame for personal gain and so for 99 out of 100 golfers there is no call for a thorough knowledge of the regulations. After all, the average golfer is unlikely to be paid to teach golf, or allow his name to be used in advertising, or make personal appearances, or sell golf equipment, or to be offered privileges or expenses to play golf. We are mostly very small fish in the golfing ocean and the nets of amateur status are designed to catch only the big sharks. The one regulation which applies to everyone is the blanket rule forbidding: *Any conduct, including activities in connection with golf gambling, which is considered detrimental to the best interests of the game.*

This rule is so sweeping in its implications that it could be invoked to cover almost any eventuality, from having one drink too many in the club bar to deliberately farming one's handicap. In practice this rule is not operated as a broad threat looming over golfers to be of good behaviour at all times. The ruling bodies do not police the game to keep its adherents on the straight-and-narrow path of righteousness. Indeed, our golfing Big Brothers do not care what we get up to provided we do not break the cardinal rule, which operates in golf just as it does in life. We must not be caught. Once our transgressions get our names into the newspapers, or create a scandal, and the good name of golf is put at risk, then – and with reluctance – Big Brother feels forced to take action. Then, the ultimate sanction is a formal notification that we have forfeited our amateur status. So what? How does that affect the average man in the street who enjoys a couple of games of golf at the weekend? In fact, the punishment can prove to be quite severe. The miscreant is thrust into a golfing limbo in which he is neither a pro nor an amateur. If he is a member of a golf club he will have to put his case to the committee. The club might decide that he should not remain a member. He would certainly not be allowed to enter competitions as an amateur, except possibly those limited to members of his club and only then with the express permission of the club. So it could well be that loss of amateur status could deprive a golfer of all the sociability of club life which makes up such a large proportion of the enjoyment of the game. He could be condemned to green-fee golf, playing at municipal courses or any clubs willing to accept him. And the process of reinstatement as an amateur, after a probationary period of exemplary amateur conduct, can be long and tedious.

Amateurism is not a subject over which we golfers need lose much sleep. The whole concept of amateurism at this point in history is outdated and the very word has come to mean something quite different from that originally intended. Today when we speak of 'amateur' we use the term pejoratively to convey a feeling of being second-rate or incompetent. The amateur in the modern sense is not so much a man who is not paid but one who is not worth paying. That view is gaining slow acceptance within golf and is expressed in that process of discussion and informal pressure which motivates the custodians of the rules. However, the process of legal reform in golf grinds exceedingly slowly.

Perhaps one day the rules will be changed to take account of modern social conditions, recognising that the day of the independently wealthy golfer who could play the game as a true amateur is past. In the meantime, the rules remain and we must all pay lip service to them, if only to the extent of following the dictum: 'Do not get caught'.

8 | COURSE BEHAVIOUR

Practice swings
Undue delay
Unseen and unheard
Rule of the road
On the green

Every copy of the Rules of Golf is prefaced by a section headed 'Etiquette'. That archaic word, which reeks of the social rituals of Victorian snobbery, is enough to switch off anyone in this egalitarian age. Golf retains this hang-over from the past out of respect for tradition, which is a worthy enough motive. But by preserving the word 'etiquette' the rulers of golf are actually nourishing the shadow of tradition while neglecting the substance of that tradition, which is the established code of good golfing behaviour. Retaining the word etiquette is counter-productive, since it offends the free spirit of contemporary golfers and puts them in quite the wrong frame of mind to accept the timeless advice under that antiquated heading. It is rather like a winemaker refusing to change his labels even though the name of his product has changed in popular usage over the years and has come to be synonymous with 'poison'. The contents may be as good as ever but it makes for problems in marketing. The custodians of golf traditions would hardly try to sell their code of golfing manners under the heading 'Snobbish mumbo-jumbo evolved by toffs to distinguish themselves from riff-raff like you and me' but that is more or less what etiquette has come to mean in the minds of most of us. So let us steam the label off the bottle and sample the contents with an open mind.

Even so, we still have to combat a certain amount of consumer resistance. Nobody likes to be lectured on how to behave. Who do these people think they are, patronising us with their rules of conduct? We already know how to behave, off the golf course or on it. The reaction may be natural but, sadly, it is not entirely valid when it comes to golf. At least, that is how it works out in practice. Theoretically, as we read the strictures on golfing behaviour in the tranquillity of our homes, we accept absolutely the words: *No player should play until the players in front are out of range.*

What could be more obvious? Who among us would deliberately seek to maim a fellow golfer? The reminder seems superfluous. Yet every day golfers are injured by drives raining down on them from behind. It is not that the act of picking up a golf club turns a man into a homicidal maniac; it is simply that on the golf course we all become so bound up in our problems, and concentrate so fiercely – as the instruction books exhort us – that we tend to be oblivious of anything else. This total preoccupation is the real justification for a written code of behaviour.

Just as we have to discipline our minds to think about the rules as we play, so we must make a positive effort to spare a thought for other players on the course. What could be more natural, on sinking a long putt, than to give vent to a whoop of delight? It is simply a harmless expression of joy. Harmless? Possibly not. Just behind the trees there may be another green, and another golfer setting himself to an equally important putt. As he takes his club back your scream of delight pierces his envelope of concentration like an electric shock. He reacts with a reflex convulsion and, in his anger, probably misses the one back. His day is spoiled.

All the rules of behaviour are based on consideration for others. And since golf is such a private activity, in essence, it is all too easy to forget about other people. That is why we all have to work on cultivating good habits so that they become second nature. Our natural instincts of consideration for other people may well become submerged in the heat of golfing battle, so we must ingrain them.

PRACTICE SWINGS

Many of the canons of behaviour have been touched upon in earlier chapters but it will do no harm to take another look at the commoner conventions and analyse the reasons for them. One of the most important concerns the practice swing. We are all perfectionists and so the commonest subject of concern in the golfer's mind as he tramps around the course is how to improve on that last shot. The urge to swing a club and get the feel of a pure stroke which will eliminate that dreadful slice, or hook, is overwhelming. We know we can do it. A couple of practice swings will put everything right. Nothing else matters. Well, one thing that certainly does matter is that fellow just over there who is about to play his shot. Our flailing away at the empty air is a distraction even if we are quite far away, a fact of which we become painfully aware when it is our turn to play and we are the victim of a human windmill out of the corner of the eye. In fact, a practice swing is of dubious benefit, except to loosen the muscles before a round. Civilised life conditions us all to abhor desecration of turf. The gardeners among us sweat to produce beautiful lawns. Public notices exhort us to keep off the grass. Subconsciously or consciously, we hate to destroy grass. Of course, if there is a golf ball sitting on it, then that is quite a different matter. That hypnotic white sphere eliminates every instinct except the desire to bash the thing a quarter of a mile. But without a ball, when the strike area is virgin turf, the natural tendency is to preserve it. The daisy is a weed, though, and there is no restraint on knocking its head off. So that becomes the target. A perfect practice swing flows through the summer air and the daisy is neatly decapitated. Now, with our muscle-memory refreshed on the execution of the perfect swing, we are ready for the ball. However, the swing that kills a daisy will – if we reproduce it exactly – catch a golf ball a glancing blow on the head. In short, the practice swing may well be the sure guarantee of a bad golf shot. The answer, you may think, is to hit down into the turf with the practice swing, and gouge out a chunk of mother earth. Well that will not make us popular with the green committee if we indulge the habit to excess. A reasonable amount of vandalism of turf is acceptable in practice swinging provided the divots are replaced although the habit should be severely restricted on the tee, particularly on the tees of short holes where iron shots are played. Greens committees have a problem maintaining teeing grounds and their job is made much more difficult if we indulge in wholesale ploughing operations with excessive practice swings. And on tees divots should not be replaced. The reason for this anomaly is that a replaced divot can provide an unstable platform from which to hit a golf ball. The ball may move just as the club-head is coming down – and that means a muffed shot for certain. If the ball is on a peg it may fall off and, as we have seen, if the downswing is completed when this happens it counts as a shot even if the club-head fails to make contact.

UNDUE DELAY

Novice golfers quickly learn that the 'correct' drill when someone else is playing a shot is to stand opposite him, clear of his range of vision and not to fidget, or make a noise. Actually, this is the procedure for a *caddie*. It would be a time-wasting ritual for players to take up this position. All that is necessary is to ensure that we are well out of the way, out of sight and out of mind of the person who is playing his shot. If he does not like having anyone behind him he is at liberty to ask us politely to move. And provided we are well out of the way there is no need to stand like a statue, with eye riveted on the player and all ready to call 'Good shot' or 'Bad luck'. There is no call for us to provide an audience for every shot. Indeed, it is often a sound policy not to watch the laboured gyrations of partners and opponents. Our own impeccable swings may become infected by the parodies of style and tempo which we observe. The only duty we have – and it is an important one, although much neglected – is to watch the flight of another player's ball so that we can give an accurate answer to his anguished question: 'Where did that one go?' For the rest, we can better spend the time while he is waggling in pondering on the initial calculations for our own shots. That way, we will be ready, once his ball is on the way, to whip out a club and let fly. Slow play is the bane of modern golf and one of the major reasons for it – we will come to more in a moment – is the time-wasting convention of switching off all thoughts of our own games while others play, and then only getting down to the job in hand when all the rest of our group are arranged into a motionless and silently admiring audience. If four players are ranged in line across a wide fairway there is no earthly reason why each of them should not be calculating the shot, selecting a club and taking up a stance more or less simultaneously. The setting up of a golf shot can be as ponderous as the loading of a Roman seige catapult, with interminable adjustments to range and aim before finally the carcass of a dead horse is hoisted into the missile-launcher. Lobbing four dead horses over the parapet takes an age, which is how it works in golf if three crews of loaders and launchers sit down and watch while the fourth goes into action. In this kind of situation the golf balls should fly into the green more as a ragged salvo. This applies even more strongly on the green, where we commonly see three players standing politely and patiently in a group at the edge of the green while the fourth player goes through his tediously mystic ritual of marking, cleaning and replacing his ball, observing the line of his putt from all four cardinal points of the compass, peering into the hole (presumably to ascertain if the aperture is large enough to accommodate a golf ball), squinting at his putter while he holds it at arm's length with finger and thumb as if it were an unexploded bomb, indulging in a lengthy series of practice swings and then shuffling interminably at the address before finally making his stroke. The process takes up to two minutes, although that is by no means a record, and by the time the short ones have been lifted and cleaned and tapped home, it is common for a four-ball to spend 10 minutes on one green.

The entire process can be streamlined if everyone does his preliminary thinking simultaneously and mentally prepares himself to step up to his putt and hit it, as soon as it is his turn. Some golfers may argue that good putting demands thorough reconnaissance and a leisurely execution. If true, then it is true only up to a point. There is clearly a limit beyond which extra fussing and fuming and fiddling actually reduces the chance of success. Some of the best putters are brisk and businesslike. Besides, there are two positive advantages in the habit of stationing yourself behind your own ball and surveying the line while another player is putting out: you eliminate watching him putt – few human activities are more tedious – and by speeding up the match you ensure more drinking time in the bar after the game.

UNSEEN AND UNHEARD

It may sound a counsel of perfection, but expletives are best deleted on the golf course, especially when playing with strangers. There are still people in these permissive days who are offended by swearing and even if we are among friends the sheer volume of our curse may carry to a neighbouring match and put somebody off his stroke. Anger, like joy, is best expressed *sotto voce*. The one time it is permitted, nay obligatory, to turn up the volume is when a wayward shot looks as if it might hit somebody, or even land near them. Then a warning shout of 'Fore!' is entirely in order, since a ruined golf shot is a fate less severe than a smack on the back of the head from a ball travelling at more than 100mph.

In essence, the conventions of golfing conduct add up to an ideal which would make it appear after our round that we had never even set foot on the course. All our divots have been invisibly mended; our footprints have been meticulously smoothed from the bunkers; no witness can be found who was on the course at the time who heard us or even, hopefully, who saw us. They were all so preoccupied with their own enjoyment that even if we came into their view we did not register on the memory. The reality is all too often far short of that ideal. An excursion round a golf course is all too often like following in the wake of a particularly undisciplined army fleeing from battle. Discarded equipment in the form of beer cans, cigarette packets and ball-wrappers litter the grass; footprints trace the progress of the rabble through the bunkers; pitch marks pock-mark the greens like Lilliputian shell craters. The culprits have affected the enjoyment of our game. The least we can do is guarantee that we do not leave a similar trail of misery for others.

RULE OF THE ROAD

It is a moot point whether it is more frustrating to be held up on the golf course by slow players ahead, or to be pushed and chivvied by impatient fast players astern. Both situations tend to make us rush our shots and therefore play badly. Certainly more bad blood is created in golf by ignorance of the rule of the road than by any other breach of convention. The word 'ignorance' is selected with some charity, since sheer bloodymindedness is often involved in a refusal to allow a faster match to go through. Normally, two-ball matches have precedence over three- and four-balls and are entitled to go through. A single player has no standing and should give way to all matches. If a match fails to keep its place on the course and loses more than one clear hole on the players in front, it should stand aside and allow the match following to pass. Those rules are quite explicit and should not raise any problems, provided everyone knows the rules. However, there is the delicate question of how to remind the slow players ahead of their duty to give us priority. An ill-tempered shout of 'Fore!' is not the answer since it is tantamount to an accusation of bad manners and is liable to be resented. If we are not invited to go through, the best way is for one of our group to go forward and politely explain that such an invitation would be appreciated. The important element is politeness and a friendly approach. If that fails, then there are no prizes for getting involved in acrimony. Better to endure the discomfort of slow play than to start a dispute which may lead to official reprimands from club officials. A quiet word with the culprits afterwards, or with an official, may prevent future breaches. The one solution to avoid is to despatch a hint in the form of hitting a ball into the sluggardly match ahead. Among some people, as court records testify, this provokes an uncontrollable urge to whack the offending ball back towards its original dispatcher, or out of bounds. Just such a sequence led one golfer to take first umbrage, then a 5-iron from his bag and finally a divot from another player's skull. A knowledge of the rule of the road plus, more importantly, an attitude of consideration for others, could save all that kind of unpleasantness.

A rather more difficult rule to follow is the one which says that any match playing a full round is entitled to pass a match playing a shorter round. The trouble here is that there is no way for the match in front to know that those following have priority. Ideally, we should all accept responsibility for calling through matches without any prompting and this means constantly being on the watch for overtaking situations. What frequently happens, of course, is that we are being held up by the match ahead and consequently we assume that it is pointless to call through a quicker match from behind. Maybe. But it is still important to get that message back to the players astern, who may be fuming at our lack of consideration. And if they still want to go through then we should allow them to do so.

The one occasion when it is absolutely essential to call through the following match is when we begin a search for a ball which is clearly not going to be found immediately. That takes precedence over all the rules of priority and two-balls should stand aside for three- and four-balls. In the same way, we should not stand on our right of way. It may be that we are playing an intense singles match of such importance that every shot must be carefully reconnoitred and each individual putt given close and lengthy attention. If we are holding up four players it is inexcusable to ignore the situation and console ourselves with the thought that we have priority. If they are patently playing faster – and they might be playing a foursome, the fastest form of golf, for all we know – then we should call them through. Both matches will benefit from that simple courtesy.

ON THE GREEN

Conduct on the green is even more important, because it is here that a trivial thoughtless action can most easily affect the outcome of the golf, if only because it is here that concentration is fiercest and the condition of the surface is most important. It is not just that an ill-timed cough can cause a putt to be missed; the anticipation of a possible interruption can be just as damaging. Hence, the need to behave at all times with the demeanour of a bishop. A proper sense of reverence should attend our actions, with due consideration for the green and for other players. So...the flagstick is removed with care so that the rim of the cup is not damaged. A sharp tug can sometimes dislodge the liner, which is another reason for the gentle approach. And when attending the flag for another player it is a good idea to ease the flag in its socket, to guarantee that it will come out smoothly. There is nothing more embarrassing than to have it jam, so you are frantically tugging at the thing. If it won't come out and his ball hits it, then he is penalised and will be in no mood to accept apologies. And when attending the flag, make sure that no shadow falls across the line of the putt and on windy days gather the folds of the flag so that its flapping will not be a distraction.

Hold the flag at arm's length to keep footprints as far from the hole as possible; there is nothing quite so maddening as to have your putt deflected from its course by a spike mark close to the edge of the cup. For the same reason, we should never walk on the line of another player's putt and this is not quite as easy as it sounds. Once a player has lifted his ball and replaced it with an almost invisible marker, the position of his line is apt to be forgotten in the preoccupation of the moment. Repairing of pitch marks is a fairly obvious duty (though all too often neglected) and it should be done with due care, lifting the impacted area with a special fork or tee-peg and then smoothing down the repair with the sole of the putter. Simply stamping on the spot, or flattening it with a putter, is not good enough. As to spike marks, we have seen that it is illegal to repair them as you putt. But *after* everyone has putted out and the flag is being carefully replaced it is only considerate to tamp down the worst examples as you move off to the next tee. Damage can also be caused to a green by dropping golf bags on it and by throwing down the flagstick. The convention of leaving golf bags off the green may be taking things rather far, since no damage is done if the thing is placed gently rather than dropped. But it is a safe practice and therefore to be encouraged. In the same way the flagstick should be placed, rather than dropped, and always in a position well clear of any possibility of its being hit by a putt.

When clubs are carried on trolleys or carts the local notices should be strictly observed. It is best always to park *behind* the green and well clear of the fringe. That way players can walk off the back of the green and the players behind can hit their approach shots immediately.

That raises the point about moving off the green without undue delay. There is no doubt that more time is wasted on the green than in any other department of golf. Although the rules allow us to mark and clean a ball for every putt it is not obligatory, even though that impression is sometimes given by pernickety professionals in tournament play. More often than not it is no less than a matter of enlightened self-interest not to clean the ball more than once (if that), as well as being an optional courtesy towards players waiting behind. And when there are people waiting to play into the green it is inexcusable to dawdle about on the green after putting out, by marking cards (better done on the next tee) or chatting, or replaying putts.

In nearly every case, a green is sited close to a tee, which is a thought to be remembered when tempted to emit a yell of delight or anguish at the fate of a putt. Plenty of golfers meticulously hold their peace while the putting is in progress and then launch into an animated post mortem as soon as the flagstick is replaced.

Companionable chatter and due expressions of congratulations or commiseration are all part of golf but always subject to the vital proviso that they do not distract other players. Remember the bishop and the due sense of reverence. For many people golf is no less than a secular religion and even if we do not share that degree of obsession we must conduct ourselves as if in a cathedral.

9 COMPETITIONS AND WAGERS

Thousands of golfers, notably in America, go through life without ever deviating from their regular custom of playing straightforward stroke-play. They have their coterie of special friends and, week in and week out, they meet to play each other. Their golf takes the form of 'matches' which are decided by a straight comparison of stroke-play scores. The one positive advantage of this custom is that within such a circle of friends the handicaps are usually mutually adjusted at frequent intervals to guarantee close encounters and keep the wager money circulating. If that is the way they like it, who are we to carp? It is none of our business. But the members of such golfing schools who exist on an unrelieved diet of stroke-play deny themselves the variety and change of pace offered by some of the different forms of the game which have survived the test of time. Most clubs organise competitions to cater for the commoner variations and the member who decides against entering them is denying himself novel golfing experiences and pleasures which can be obtained in no other way, particularly in foursomes golf, mixed or otherwise, which produces a whole new range of problems, anxieties and stresses.

In this chapter we will look at the special rules and conditions covering these speciality events.

BOGEY AND PAR COMPETITIONS

The term 'bogey' is fast disappearing from all but the most traditional of clubs and in America the word is now used almost exclusively in its modern sense to describe a score of one over par for a hole. But it still lingers on elsewhere in its archaic sense as the target score which should be taken at any hole by a scratch player. It thus differs slightly from 'par' which is defined as the score which a first-class player should take on any hole *in summer conditions*. In most places par is computed on a strictly mathematical basis according to the length of each hole (up to 250 yards, par-3; 251–475 yards, par-4; 476 yards and over, par-5). So when clubs persist with the obsolescent bogey system their cards have separate columns to denote the par rating for each hole and the bogey score (which is usually the same as par except that the longer and more difficult par-4s become bogey-5s). For the sake of simplicity let us forget about bogey and talk only in terms of par competitions. The rules, of course, are identical and the aim is to play a match against an invisible opponent in the form of par. The winner is the player who can finish the most holes up on Old Man Par.

The first pitfall for the uninitiated is that although you are playing a match, hole by hole, this form of golf is played according to the rules of stroke-play. That sounds confusing but is really quite logical. The variations in the rules for match-play are all concerned with the presence of an opponent – what happens if he plays your ball, or if you steal his honour. In a par competition there is no physical enemy, merely a tyrannical figure which you have to equal or beat on each hole. Par cannot intervene in the contest so you are on your own, just as in stroke-play. Therefore you play stroke-play rules. You get an allowance of three-quarters of your handicap, as in match-play, and your marker is responsible only for recording your gross score at each hole. It is up to the committee to mark the holes at which you receive strokes and to work out your final standing against par. However, you will be well aware of the holes where you get a handicap stroke and once you have played so many shots that it is no longer possible to get even a half against par then you should pick up your ball and leave a blank in the space for that hole's score. The committee will accept such blanks as a loss to par.

STABLEFORDS

In 1931 Dr Frank Stableford of Liverpool invented the Stableford system of scoring and his novel competition proved so enduringly popular that in 1968 this form of golf was given official blessing by being incorporated into the rules of golf. Stablefords are essentially the same as par competitions, using the same stroke-play rules and conventions and with individual competitors usually getting an allowance of seven-eighths of handicap. (This can be varied by the committee and is not governed by a rule of golf.) Remember that in computing these allowances that a fraction of a half, or more, counts as a full stroke. Fractions smaller than a half count nothing. Again your only duty is to see that your marker records your gross score for each hole. The committee works out your total on the basis of Dr

Stableford's system by awarding one point for every hole completed in a net score of one over par; two points for par; three points for a birdie and so on. The advantage of this method over conventional par and bogey competitions is that it graduates the field more finely. Where a par competition might produce four joint winners all standing three-up on par, their identical scores could well produce an outright winner if their play were computed by Stableford points.

FOURSOMES

Golf is essentially an individual game and the closest it comes to involving the camaraderie and interdependence of team games is in foursomes. For that reason alone – although there are others – it is a pity that many golfers never play foursomes, or Scotch Foursomes as it is commonly known in America. It is commonplace for seasoned professionals and leading amateurs to admit, on being selected for international teams, that this will be their first experience of foursomes. Basically, it is partner golf with each pair playing one ball in alternate strokes. It is officially match-play but this form can also be used in stroke-play or Stablefords. Each partnership decides in advance which of the pair shall drive at the 1st tee. From then on they drive alternately. Thus one player always drives on the odd-numbered holes, his partner at the even, regardless of who may have sunk the last putt on the previous green. During the play of each hole the partners take alternate shots at their joint ball and penalty strokes do not affect this order of play. If a player accidentally plays out of turn – this sometimes happens in the heat of the moment when a player putts up to the lip of the hole and then unthinkingly taps it in – then that stroke is cancelled, the ball is replaced and the side incurs two penalty strokes.

GREENSOMES

Among golfing societies and similar gatherings of like-minded enthusiasts who may have widely varying handicaps, and who may also have indulged themselves freely with cheering spirits over lunch, a popular though unofficial variation on foursomes for a light-hearted afternoon romp is the greensome. The only difference here is that both partners drive at each hole and then select which of their two drives they prefer to play out in alternate shots. A greensome-Stableford is a popular form, with partners receiving three-eighths of the difference in their combined handicaps, just as in foursomes.

THREE-BALLS AND VARIATIONS

We are now getting into deepish water and must be quite sure of our terminology. A three-ball is when three players go out and each man plays a separate match against two separate opponents. Thus there are three distinct matches involved and this type of golf should not be confused with a threesome. This is a match in which a single player competes against a partnership playing alternate shots at the same ball under the same conditions as for foursomes golf.

There are several other variations (unofficial) of enjoyable three-man golf and we might mention two of them. Strictly speaking they are not different forms of golf so much as scoring conventions for the purpose of wagering. Chairman is played to three-ball rules and the first player to win a hole outright is declared to be in the chair. If then, on the next hole, he again wins outright from both opponents he collects the prearranged wager for winning a hole. He remains in the chair if the subsequent hole results in a half with either or both of his opponents but he does not collect any wager. When one of the other two players wins a hole outright he then becomes the new chairman. It can be seen, then, that a player has to win two holes, possibly separated by halves, before he can collect any wager.

The other three-man convention is also match-play and here six points are available on each hole. Perhaps the best way to explain how the points are divided is by example. If B and C both fail to complete a hole then A gets all six points. If A wins a hole, and B and C halve it, then the split is four points to A and one apiece to B and C. If A and B halve, both beating C, then A and B get three points apiece, and C zero. If all halve they get two points each. Finally, if A beats B who in turn beats C, then A gets four points, B two points and C nothing. It sounds rather complicated when put like that but in practice is quite simple and quickly mastered. In order to keep it simple as you go along, and avoid having to keep a written tally of the totals, it is usual after each hole to reduce the lowest score to zero. Thus if *A* wins the first hole outright from *B* and *C*, who halve, the scores would be: *A* = 4, *B* = 1, *C* = 1. Now on the second hole *A* and *C* halve, both beating *B*, *A* and *C* collect three points apiece so the aggregates now read: *A* = 7, *B* = 1, *C* = 4. Reduce poor *B's* total to zero by subtracting one point all round and proceed to the third tee with the scores at: *A* = 6, *B* = 0, *C* = 3. Again it sounds complicated but you soon get the hang of it.

BEST BALL

This is a rare form of match-play golf and is normally used only when a very good player is in the company of two lesser performers. The tiger plays against the better ball of the two rabbits. Best-ball golf can be played against two or three opponents and obviously requires very careful negotiation in the matter of handicapping before any wager is struck. Normally, no handicap allowance is made at all unless the good player is very sure of himself, such as a pro playing against two long-handicap members.

FOUR-BALL MATCH-PLAY

Much commoner is the four-ball match in which partners pit their better ball against the better ball of their opponents. One point to be made about this form of golf is that partners play as a 'side' and this varies the general rule about the ball furthest from the hole to be played first. Here it is the side with a ball furthest from the hole which has the option of selecting which of their two balls is to be played first. If a side plays out of turn the opponents may immediately require the shot to be replayed in correct order and without penalty. That provision caused much bitterness in the Ryder Cup match at Royal Birkdale in 1969 when the American pair of Ken Still and Dave Hill putted out of turn. They were duly 'called' by their opponents and took umbrage. In the absence of a firm and speedy ruling as to their rights, the Americans conceded the hole in the face of what they considered to be rulesmanship. The match was played out in high tension and the incident serves to underline the necessity for a sound grasp of the laws and the need to approach disputes with cool detachment. Here the Americans lost a hole which they could have saved by accepting their right to re-putt without penalty.

There are a few other special provisions for this form of golf. Any player can have any ball lifted and if a player's ball moves any other ball in the match, the owner of the moved ball must replace it, without penalty. The most important provision is that if a player's infringement of a rule might help his partner, or adversely affect the other side, then *both* partners incur the relevant penalty. In all other cases an accidental breach of rule does not call down a penalty on the partner.

An example may help to clarify this principle. If your ball is deflected by one of your opponents then his side loses the hole, both opponents being penalised because your side was adversely affected. But if you move your ball in lifting a loose impediment, then you suffer the penalty but your partner who cannot possibly benefit from your action – does not.

Handicapping for four-ball matches is best settled by reducing the lowest handicap player to scratch, thus giving him no strokes. He is called the back marker and this eliminates the absurd possibility of all four players getting a handicap stroke at the same hole. Say the back marker is a 6-handicap player. The others get threequarters of the difference between their handicaps and 6. So if a four-ball match consisted of players with handicaps of 6, 12, 16 and 20 the differences would be 0, 6, 10 and 14 and three-quarter allowances would produce 0 strokes, 5 strokes, 8 strokes and 11 strokes (don't forget the fraction rule: half or more counts a stroke, less than a half counts nothing).

ECLECTICS

These are run over a period of time, such as the months of winter, and require a number of stroke-play cards to be returned. Some clubs put no limit on the number of cards which may be returned and this form of competition can produce a useful source of revenue if a separate entry fee is required for each card. At the end of the allotted time the committee sorts through the cards of each competitor and extracts the lowest score returned for each individual hole. It is, incidentally, a great boost to the morale of a veteran club member to work out his lifetime eclectic for his home course. Over a number of years he will have had eagles at most holes, or perhaps better, and quite moderate golfers run up eclectic scores in the low forties. For a man who has never broken 90 on his own course that can be a most comforting thought.

ROUND ROBINS

Unless a club has a really energetic competition secretary, plus good luck, Round Robins tend to be cumbersome and inconclusive affairs. The theory is that each entrant meets everyone else at match-play and the winner is the one who scores most wins. It is a good method of getting the members known to each other but illness and other emergencies can play havoc with the timetable. Provision has to be made for players to concede matches and it is not really satisfactory for a contest to be decided on a number of inevitable concessions.

LIMITED-CLUB COMPETITIONS

A popular novelty which has rather fallen into disuse is the limited-club event. This can take many forms, as the name suggests. A seven-club competition calls for a fair degree of advance planning by the contestants, although not nearly so much preliminary anguish as the competitions in which you are limited to a putter and one other club. The revealing aspect about these events is that the level of scoring is often almost as good as in the club's regular stroke-play competitions. In Europe there is a professional tournament for which the entrants are limited to a 4 iron only. On every occasion on which is has been played the winning score has been below par.

PRO-AMS

Many club golfers are diffident about entering for pro-ams on the grounds that they are not good enough to compete in such illustrious company, possibly watched by scornful spectators, and they are apprehensive about making fools of themselves. The fear may be natural enough, and quite understandable, but it has absolutely no validity so far as the professionals are concerned. Do not be afraid of embarrassing your pro. He does not want to play with the low-handicap tigers. They are no good to him. In most pro-ams three amateurs play off handicap and when any of them produces a better net score than the pro on any hole then that is the score to count.

The 1 handicap player has comparatively little chance of improving on the professional's score. In the natural order of things they will both get par figures on most of the holes. The long-handicap men are the useful partners. You, with your generous stroke allowance, will surely get par figures on some of the holes. And if your handicap strokes fall at those holes you will contribute a birdie every time. So do not be diffident on the score that you will be no more than a passenger, providing light relief for the others. You will not be that and you will almost certainly benefit your golf from the advice and encouragement of your pro. As for the danger of provoking uncontrolled merriment among the crowd, such fears are almost totally illusory. As an amateur, people expect you to hit bad shots and once you have exceeded your ration on any hole you can save your blushes by picking up your ball. What is more, as you can console yourself, your bad shots serve to emphasise the skill of your professional. Your black despair is the background against which the diamond of his brilliance is supposed to be contrasted. In any case, most of the time spectators ignore the laboured efforts of the amateurs and have eyes only for the professionals. So if you get the chance, get our there and enjoy yourself. The only warning which is necessary is not to delude yourself before the round that perhaps you will have one of those golden days when everything goes right and you play well above your normal form. That never happens. You always play worse than you thought possible but pro-ams can still be great fun for all that.

GAMBLING

The ruling bodies of golf lay down pious policies on gambling although in their role as custodians of tradition they are on slightly uneasy ground here. Since the earliest recorded minutes of club affairs back in the eighteenth century gambling has played an integral part in golf, to the extent that the clubs maintained 'Bett books'. A special officer was elected to record challenges made at the roisterous club dinners so that there would be written proof when the dawn brought its customary hangover and partial amnesia over the previous evening's bargains. What the legislators really seek to control is the scope of gambling, rather than the fact of it. There is no doubt that big-money wagers, Calcutta sweepstakes and auction pools can put a severe strain on the ideal of golf as a game of trust and can create suspicion and discord within a club. And as soon as big money becomes involved the spirit of the rules of amateur status is thoroughly compromised. As an amateur you may not accept a golf prize with a retail value of more than £300 or $500 in parts of Europe and areas under the jurisdiction of the United States Golf Association. There is nothing that the authorities can do to stop you having a fat bundle on a private match, which is why they do not even try to prevent it. But as soon as an organised competition is involved, over which the authorities have some control, then they can and do exert a degree of pressure, albeit mostly moral.

You may feel, in passing, that as the winner of a competition you are put into a highly invidious position by your responsibility instantly to appraise the retail value of your prize and then, with as much disdain as you can muster, hand it back if it exceeds the limit. There are steely characters capable of acting with such lofty self-righteousness but for the majority of us frail vessels the euphoria of the occasion, combined with the sheer embarrassment of the alternative, would dull any pricking of conscience. We would, in short, grab the loot and hope the authorities did not get to hear about it. Can we be blamed?

Well, the authorities can and do blame any culprit on whom they can pin a rap. Golfers have been deprived of their amateur status, which thus precludes them from competing in further official competitions. In practice, this is an intolerable responsibility to place on the individual golfer and the authorities would do better to put the onus on competition organisers, over whom they have a measure of control, not to award prizes over the limit.

As for gambling in private golf, nobody cares what you

get up to, except possibly your dependants. It is entirely up to you but from a purely golfing point of view it is bad to play for more than you can afford to lose without wincing. That piece of advice might possibly be reversed in the case of young professionals who must learn to play under exceptional stresses; they should always play for a bit more than they can comfortably afford to lose.

For the novice amateur, however, the problem is to work out in advance exactly how high his gambling liability might be. A few of the conventions of golf wagering should be thoroughly absorbed to avoid future distress.

The Nassau is a popular, universal bet. It means that the agreed sum is really trebled. A 'golf-ball Nassau' involves one golf ball on the result of the first nine holes, another ball on the second nine holes and a third ball on the overall result. In four-ball matches the expression 'corner' is much used and frequently misunderstood. It means that the agreed bet is due from both partners, not the joint responsibility of the partnership. Thus if you lose a bet for 'a golf ball a corner' in a four-ball you will be expected to hand over a ball and so will your partner. Just to complicate matters some people use the word 'corner' in the sense of exactly double the above liability. In their terms 'a golf ball a corner' means that both losing partners give a ball apiece to both winners. Since there is no official rule, or definition, it is important to get this situation straightened out before the match. The best plan is to avoid the word 'corner' and agree on the liability for the side. After all, it is just as easy to say 'two golf balls a side'. Then everyone knows exactly what is at stake.

Much more potentially dangerous is the word 'press'. The convention of a press is that a side which becomes two holes down in a match can press their opponents. That starts a secondary bet over the remaining holes and can be followed in due course by yet another press. Simple mathematics shows that a straight bet of one golf ball 'with automatic presses' could cost a side nine balls if the partnership lost every hole. Care is also needed to ensure that everyone understands the same press convention. Some people have a rule that you can only press for half the original stake; others press for the full amount. It could be important for you to know which system you are playing.

If you imagine that it would not be possible to get more complicated than a match with, say, three presses going at once, then you would be vastly mistaken. In four-ball golf it is quite common to have the main partnership bet, with automatic presses, and for all the players to be involved in individual matches with each of the other three players at the same time, again with automatic presses, Now you can be getting into really rich country, even if the basic bet is only one golf ball. Add up the possibilities. Have a really bad day and you could find yourself liable to pay up three-dozen golf balls. Translate that into terms of wagering a week's rent and you can appreciate the kind of mess that it is possible to get into by agreeing to a bet you do not fully understand.

The soundest rule in golf gambling is to play it safe and keep it simple. A modest flutter may well add spice to the match but the moment anyone starts mentioning side bets and presses the best advice is to announce your limit and stick to it. You can always console yourself with the noble thought that you are acting within the spirit of the rules of amateur status.

10 | DECISIONS AND DISPUTES

RULE 1: THE GAME

This is the catch-all rule which can be invoked for a wide range of violations in situations not covered by the other rules. That statement may sound contradictory, for if a situation is not covered by a rule of golf it self-evidently cannot involve a punishable breach. The key that unlocks this enigma is the word 'equity'. Rule 1.(4) says that if any point in dispute is not covered by the Rules, the decision shall be made in accordance with equity. We must be careful how we interpret that word. It does not mean common sense, or natural justice, or sportsmanship, or the spirit of the game. In this context equity has a narrow and specific meaning. It is impossible for the legislators to anticipate every contingency which might be met in the course of a five-mile walk across country. Nor can they foresee every nuance of human folly and depravity of which golfers are capable. As it is, golf law – including the fat volume of Decisions – runs close to 200,000 words. So we may define equity as the state of mind which produced that mass of rules and decisions. A ruling under equity is what the Rules of Golf committee would have embodied in golf law if it had foreseen the particular dispute arising from a situation so freakish that it was not already covered by the comprehensive code of golf law.

A ruling in equity will not necessarily be equitable in the sense that the average man on top of a number 11 omnibus understands the word. So if a situation arises for which the rules of golf provide no solution, do not ask yourself 'What is fair in this instance?' Ask instead 'What was the intention behind the rule which is concerned with this general situation?'

Bearing that stricture in mind, see if you can resolve the problem involved in Decision 1. (4)/1: 'Q. As A was making his backswing, B accidentally dropped a ball which rolled within six inches of A's ball. The appearance of the dropped ball startled A, causing him to top his shot. In equity, should A be permitted to replay the stroke? How do you rule? The official decision was: *No. Distractions are a common occurrence which players must accept.* Had B deliberately dropped that ball with the intention of putting his opponent off his stroke then he would have been liable for disqualification as a serious breach of Rule 1.(2).

In the author's view it is a weakness of the rules that the penalty of disqualification covers such a wide range of violations, from downright cheating to the unconscious aberration of failing to notice that your marker has put you down for a wrong score on one hole. The word 'disqualification' carries a stigma, appropriately enough in the game of golf, implying violations involving an intention to take an unfair advantage. But no such stigma should attach to disqualifications for purely technical breaches made in all innocence. Perhaps golf could devise a new penalty which carries the same effect but a less shameful title, such as 'Lapsed Card'.

The Decision on the Rules of Golf are published in book form and revised regularly. Serious golfers, and not so serious golfers too, are advised to subscribe to the Decisions service and keep the book handy for idle moments. The Decisions make entertaining and interesting light reading but they also provide an insight into the intention behind the rules which will stand the golfer in good stead.

Take Decision 1.(1)/3 for example. 'Q. At a par-3 hole a player, believing his original ball may be lost, plays a provisional ball. He searches for five minutes for the original ball and then plays the provisional ball on to the green. At that point the original ball is found in the hole. What is the ruling? A. The player's score is 1. The play of the hole was completed when the player holed the original ball.' Incidentally, a verbal concession of the hole would not have changed the ruling. A concession cannot supersede the facts (Decision 2. (4)/11).

Another slightly unexpected point is raised by Decision 1. (2)/6. 'Q. As a gesture of sportsmanship, a player removes a loose impediment in a hazard, thus improving the lie of his opponent's ball. The player's ball was not in the hazard. What is the ruling?' Surely, you may feel, an act of kindness cannot be a sin. Similarly, a generous spirit might say: 'You are not allowed to tap down that intrusive spike mark on the line of your putt but since it does not affect my putt in any way, I will tap it down for you.' Beware of benevolent urges. If you want to be bountiful concede the putt, or the hole, but do not monkey about with the lawful procedures of the game. This is what the Rules of Golf Committee decree: 'A. Under Rule 1-2 the player incurs a penalty of loss of hole.' Thus curdles the milk of human kindness.

Decisions on Rule 1 also establish the principle that a golfer is not obliged to risk physical danger in playing a stroke nor to put other people or animals in danger. So if there is a real risk, such as your ball lying near a venomous snake or by a bird's nest, you drop in a similar lie clear of the danger. You will not be penalised for unduly delaying play if you wait while people or animals on your line of fire move to safety.

RULE 2: MATCH-PLAY

Many of the Decisions on Rule 2 are concerned with concessions. If two important points are kept in mind such problems should not arise.

> 1 Always make a concession in unambiguous terms, preferably picking up your opponent's ball and handing it to him as you do so.
>
> 2 Remember that a concession cannot override a fact. But a concession cannot be declined or withdrawn, so if your opponent's ball stops on the lip and he concedes the hole he cannot claim a half if his ball subsequently topples into the hole.

If a dispute arises it has to be settled there and then and the most civilised way of doing so is to agree to halve the hole. After all, golf is a game, not a battle of life and death.

RULE 3: STROKE-PLAY

The golfer has to be his own policeman, prosecutor, judge and jury, but there will be many occasions when a player is unsure of the correct procedure to be followed. Often a fellow competitor will give his opinion, but we must be wary of such 'rulings'. He may have got it all wrong and it will cut no ice with the committee if you plead that you acted in accordance with the advice of an experienced companion. It is much safer in doubtful cases to take advantage of the special stroke-play provision for playing a second ball. You play your original ball as it lies and drop a second ball in the place where you may be allowed to obtain relief. Play out both balls and let the committee sort out the legalities.

RULE 4: CLUBS

Most people assume, reasonably enough, that clubs made by a reputable manufacturer will conform to the specifications in the Rules of Golf. In 1984 the specifications were varied to permit the use of U-shaped grooves in club-faces in addition to the traditional V-grooves. An American manufacturer brought out a model with U-grooves and a rancorous dispute broke out with the United States Golf Association about the dimensions of the grooves and the distance between them, It was literally a hair-splitting argument because the disputed measurement amounted to no more than half the width of a human hair. The USGA then adopted its own invented system of measurement, of no engineering pedigree, called the thirty degree method, which it claimed rendered the disputed clubs non-conforming. The Royal and Ancient Golf Club at St Andrews adopted these measures in a spirit of co-operation and for the sake of uniformity of rules. Faced by a potentially ruinous law suit the USGA then did a U-turn on U-grooves and announced that the non-conforming clubs would be deemed to be conforming. The Royal and Ancient did no such about-turn and so we currently have the situation in which one set of clubs is legal in the United States and Mexico but not in the rest of the world. In time uniformity will be achieved again, because the manufacturer has revised the design and those non-conforming models will disappear through natural replacement. For the moment it is a sensible precaution if a player has the slightest doubt about the legality of his irons to submit them to the committee for checking before an important competition.

This lengthy, divisive and expensive dispute could have been avoided if the ruling bodies had followed standard engineering procedure when they introduced the new specifications by defining an appropriate tolerance for this type of manufacture. One five-thousandth of an inch tolerance would have saved yards and yards of legal submissions and many gallons of bad blood.

RULE 5: THE BALL

The player is responsible for the legality of his equipment yet, in the case of the ball, he has no way of testing it because the only machine for doing so is housed at the United States Golf Association headquarters in Far Hills, New Jersey. The USGA regularly tests all brands of golf ball and issues a list of conforming balls. One of the fundamental principles of golf is therefore violated by the body entrusted to preserve it, and all the player can do is confirm that his ball appears on the approved list.

Rule 5-3 details the manner and conditions for substituting a damaged ball during the play of a hole. (The ball may be changed at will once a played has holed out.) Substituting a ball which has become unfit for play is probably the most abused rule in golf; in professional tournament golf it is almost as if there is a tacit agreement to ignore the provisions of this rule.

It is commonplace for a golfer who has just played a recovery shot from sand to call across the fairway to his marker or a fellow competitor announcing that he proposes to change his ball. Often enough even this minimal nod in the directions of the provisions of 5-3 is neglected. After marking and lifting a ball on the green, especially after a bunker shot, a caddie can frequently be seen returning a different ball to the player. A scuffed surface is not reason enough to substitute a ball; it must be visibly cut, cracked or out of shape, and the player must announce to his marker or fellow competitor his intention of lifting a ball to inspect its fitness for play and provide an opportunity for its examination. From observation of the game's shop window competitions it is clear that the authorities make precious little attempt to enforce 5-3 and if a rule has fallen into disuse it should be revised or rescinded. After all, if one rule is widely believed to be so onerous that it is universally ignored, it is a short stop on the slippery path towards treating other rules with a similar lack of respect.

RULE 6: THE PLAYER

It is not necessary for the proper enjoyment of the game to be an authority on the rules of golf provided a copy of the Rules is carried for reference over doubtful points of procedure. But Rule 6 covers the responsibilities of the player and should be thoroughly learned and digested. Fortunately the provisions of Rule 6 are clear and easily absorbed, being mainly common sense. In one particular a civilised convention of golf will help to make the game the enjoyable experience it is supposed to be. The rule merely states that match-play opponents must declare their correct handicaps. It often happens, however, than an inexperienced golfer will forget in the excitement of the moment where he is entitled to a handicap stroke. He may reflect ruefully, although not audibly for preference, that if only he had realised he was entitled to a handicap stroke he would have played the hole differently. The obvious response, again not to be uttered aloud in polite company, is: 'Damn fool, you, for not checking your card on the tee'.

The cause of these regrettable events can be eliminated if, as the player with the lower handicap, you adopt the habit of announcing on every occasion: 'You get a stroke on this hole'. The rules do not require you to make this sporting gesture but your victory will be all the sweeter if you have given your opponent every consideration.

The duties of a marker are not closely defined in Rule 6, beyond stating that a marker is not a referee. A marker is not required to accompany the player into the woods and monitor his every despairing hack or even to keep count of a succession of expletives. If from your observation the player has miscounted the number of strokes he has played you may recall his play with him and agree the correct score. But your only duty is to record the score the player tells you. If you believe it to be wrong, and you cannot reconcile the difference of opinion, you are at liberty to refuse to sign his card. It is the duty of the committee to adjudicate. In fairness, a marker should inform the player that he proposes not to sign the card.

RULE 7: PRACTICE

If you are one of those people who insist on filling every waking moment by hitting something with a golf club you should confine your obsession to fir cones and acorns, otherwise you will land yourself with a penalty sooner or later. Study Rule 7 which makes some provision for hitting practice shots between holes. But restrain yourself during play of a hole. Decisions make a couple of concessions: practice balls which stray on to the course from the driving range may be chipped off the playing area; and if you are making a practice swing in the rough and happen to dislodge an unsuspected ball then this does not count as a practice stroke.

RULE 8: ADVICE

The definition of 'advice' can be misleading – a semantic minefield through which the reader must pick his way gingerly, word by word. A casual reading implies that 'advice' is any statement which could influence a player in making up his mind how to tackle a hole or plan a stroke. Such is far from the case. You are free to ask anyone for information that is publicly available; everything you need to determine your play. You can, for instance, ask the length of the hole, which way it dog-legs, whether there is a ditch over that brow, whether a distance marker is accurate, how close your opponent's ball lies from the flagstick, whether his ball is a hazard, how far the drive must be carried through the air to reach the fairway; and so on. What you must not do is ask or give advice on what club to use or how to swing it. That advice may only be exchanged between a player, his partner or their caddies. If you absolutely must know what club an opponent or fellow competitor has just used you are free to look at it as he returns it to his bag. If the devious swine immediately drops a towel over his clubs to foil your inquisitiveness then that's that. If you remove the towel to take a peek you are in breach of Rule 8-1 and liable to two penalty strokes or loss of hole.

RULE 9: INFORMING OF STROKES TAKEN

This is essentially a match-play rule and simply labours the point, as if you needed any reminding, that you must show an opponent due consideration at all times. So you inform him as soon as practicable if you incur a penalty stroke, and you give him the correct information when he asks how many strokes you have taken. If you give wrong information and fail to correct it before your opponent plays his next stroke you lose the hole.

RULE 10: ORDER OF PLAY

Many problems arise when golfers ignore a rule on the basis that 'It makes no difference'. Often enough, but by no means always, it makes no difference in which order shots are played, especially in stroke-play. For instance, it may happen – and indeed did happen on one occasion – that the player with the honour excused himself to go to the toilet. In the interests of maintaining the pace of play, a fellow competitor decided that it would make no difference if he played his shot. It did make a difference: he was penalised. The rule was subsequently changed, and there is not a penalty now for playing out of turn in stroke-play (unless players collude to give one of them an advantage). The best policy is to play to the rules, all of the rules, all of the time. In match-play if you play out of turn your opponent may require you to replay the stroke, and that involves a form of unofficial penalty because in your embarrassment you may well make a hash of your replayed shot.

Decision 10-1c/2 demonstrates the 'makes no difference' syndrome. A player asked his opponent to lift his ball which lay on the line of the player's putt. Instead of complying with the request, the opponent putted out of turn. After all, it made no difference. The ruling was that the player had the right to insist that the opponent replay his putt in the correct order. In stroke-play you do have the option to lift or putt out in this situation.

RULE 11: TEEING GROUND

It is quite astonishing how many golfers tee their balls on the extreme forward limit of the teeing ground, as if that last vital half-inch could possibly make any difference on a final shot. It is a stupid habit, indicating either that you are obsessive about length and are liable to overswing, or that you are seeking an 'edge', branding yourself as someone who will bear careful watching. Tee the ball well inside the limits and an easy conscience will pay dividends in an easy swing.

When your ball is on a tee peg it is not in play until you have made a stroke at it. That is why there is no penalty if you dislodge the ball from its perch as you are addressing it, or if it topples as you are making your upswing. You re-tee it and start again. But beware of this privilege. Say you have an air shot and as you are addressing the ball for your second attempt you dislodge it. That is a penalty stroke 11-3/1 because the ball is now in play.

On the next tee you have a fractional improvement in form and your drive catches the ball the slightest of glancing blows, enough to cause it to fall off its tee-peg but not enough to propel it out of the teeing ground. That is a tiny grain of comfort, you reflect, because being within the teeing ground you can tee it up again for your next attempt. Wrong! The ball is now in play and you must not move it 11-3/2.

Your horrendous round continues and at the next hole you have the satisfaction of catching your ball flush, albeit that the ball goes out of bounds. Your playing companion then points out that you had teed your ball outside the teeing ground. You reload, in golfing parlance, tee up another ball within the teeing ground and hit off. 'That's three penalty strokes!' you moan, 'Two for playing from outside the teeing ground, and one for stroke and distance'. Your wise and kindly playing companion brings a shred of solace. 'No, the ball played from outside the teeing ground was not in play. Therefore the fact that it came to rest out of bounds was irrelevant and the stroke itself did not count' 11-4b/6.

RULE 12: SEARCHING FOR AND IDENTIFYING BALL

In general, the purpose of the rules is to make provision for the round to be completed in the face of the many complications which may be encountered while traversing four or five miles of the countryside. The rules are not concerned to make the game easier for you. So you should be extremely wary of doing anything which gives you a positive benefit. Some perfectly lawful procedures do so, but you should be meticulous in checking that the beneficial procedure you are contemplating really is lawful. First of all you must be absolutely sure of the facts. The condition in which your ball lies is, without any scintilla of doubt, casual water. Fine. Go ahead and take the appropriate relief. But, you may feel, you will make doubly sure by checking with your opponent or marker. Bear in mind the Sunningdale rule, however, a convention that asking for confirmation is an admission of doubt, and if you ask the answer has to be 'No'. Play the Sunningdale rule and over a golfing lifetime it may cost you a few strokes, but this will undoubtedly save you the embarrassment and disappointment of many penalty strokes.

By the same token, there will be occasions when you will unwittingly infringe a rule and have to call a penalty on yourself. This is not an occasion for a self-righteous display of your piety and honesty. Calling a penalty on yourself is not an act of virtue; it is no more than refraining from picking your friends' pockets. You have to tell your opponent or marker when you have incurred a penalty stroke but don't make a meal of it.

RULE 13: BALL PLAYED AS IT LIES

The rules of golf are predicated on the assumption that you will devote all your ingenuity to cheating at every opportunity. That is why we have such a mass of legislation. The authorities have tried to anticipate every possible contingency for taking an unfair advantage and have framed a rule to prohibit it. The essence of golf can be expressed in fewer than a dozen basic rules, and Rule 13 is one of them: *The ball shall be played as it lies*. Originally the only exception to this fundamental principle were procedures which enabled you to continue your round. Then the ruling bodies introduced exceptions which provided relief simply because you had an unfavourable lie, in the mistaken belief that they were making the game fairer when, in fact, they were penalising skill.

Most Rule 13 infringements involve the clause forbidding the improvement of your lie, area of intended swing or line of play. In particular it is worth reading the Decisions to get a full understanding of what is meant by *fairly taking a stance*. You must not move, bend or break anything growing or fixed except as may occur in fairly taking a stance. The best interpretation of this rule as you plunge into the undergrowth is to dismiss from your mind all considerations of how you can play your shot and to concentrate solely on bending or moving such branches and shrubbery as are necessary for you to take a stance. So, unless you cannot stand to the ball without doing so, you must not hook an inconvenient branch behind your leg.

Another pitfall is the provision against testing the surface of a hazard. For some inscrutable reason this prohibition even extends to the water in a water hazard. It may be a contradiction in terms to talk of 'grounding' your club in water but you must not do it.

RULE 14. STRIKING THE BALL

What happens if you make a swing and the club head passes harmlessly over the ball, in other words, an air shot? Do you count that as a stroke? Yes you do. But if you check your downswing before it strikes the ball then technically that does not constitute a stroke.

RULE 15: PLAYING A WRONG BALL

A golf ball can appear in many guises. It can be the ball in play, a wrong ball, a lost ball, a second ball, a provisional ball, an opponent's ball, a ball out of play, an outside agency, a fellow competitor's ball, or a movable obstruction. It will greatly help in the learning and application of the rules if you can sort out this load of balls and distinguish one from the other.

RULE 16: THE PUTTING GREEN

Mankind is divided into two groups, those who would sooner cut off a hand rather than repair a spike mark and those who repair spike marks surreptitiously while pretending to do something else. The spike mark rule is an anomaly since we can repair other man-made damage to the green, pitch marks, sunken hole plugs and damaged hole rims. Since legislation cannot change human nature it would make sense to permit repair of all imperfections on the line of your putt, or none of them. That way we would all be playing the same game at least.

RULE 17: THE FLAGSTICK

Here we have another case of a rule for the sake of rules. Slow play, the bane of modern golf, would speed up if the whole, superfluous rigmarole of flagstick legislation were rescinded. It makes no contribution to the game of golf but until the day of enlightenment dawns there is nothing else for it but to commit the rules to memory.

RULE 18. BALL AT REST MOVED

If we are to take the rules absolutely literally, as we are earnestly enjoined so to do, then nobody plays the game properly. Rule 18-2a(ii) states: *When a player's ball is in play, if equipment of the player…causes the ball to move, the player shall incur a penalty stroke.* Clear as daylight, isn't it? When you hit your ball with your club you count one stroke and add one penalty stroke. That turns your usual 72 into 144. You may think 'What's the difference?' Everyone has to double his score so you still win the kitty. Not at all. By signing for a 72 when your true score was 144 you are automatically disqualified. All those trophies, green jackets and fat cheques will have to be sent back.

RULE 19: BALL IN MOTION DEFLECTED OR STOPPED

The rules of golf take precedence over the laws of nature, demonstrable facts and common sense. In applying Rules 18 and 19 a ball which is patently in motion, may be legally at rest (ie in flowing water, when teetering on the lip of a hole, or when wedged in the bough of a waving tree). Likewise, wind has no status in the rules. It is not an outside agency. So if you play to the green of a short hole with your tee shot, mark the ball and lift it, put it in your pocket for five minutes while your fellow competitor holes out, replace it, lift your marker and if, before addressing your ball, the wind blows it into the hole, then the rules say, in effect, that when your ball came to rest it stored away some energy and its subsequent movement into the hole was actually a continuation of its flight from the tee. You have your hole in one. Men have been canonised for lesser miracles than those performed by the Rules of Golf committees.

RULE 20: LIFTING, DROPPING AND PLACING

This is among the most important rules in the book. Learn it thoroughly, read and digest the Decisions and, if you meet a situation which raises a scintilla of doubt, play the ball as it lies.

RULE 21: CLEANING BALL

Avoid making a fetish of playing with a pristine golf ball. The rules allow you to clean your ball on the green before each putt and through the green when taking relief. But it is not obligatory to clean your ball on every lawful occasion, nor is it necessary. Those lordly tournament stars who lift a ball and clean it before a two-inch tap-in do golf a great disservice by their time-wasting posturing. Impressionable spectators get the idea that it helps and copy the absurd ritual. One clean per green is a sensible rule to adopt, and then only if the ball has mud on it.

RULE 22: BALL INTERFERING WITH OR ASSISTING PLAY

This is one rule which has been greatly improved and simplified. You can lift your ball at any time if you think it might assist any other player, and have any ball lifted if it might interfere with your play or help someone else's. In stroke-play, if you are asked to lift your ball you have the option of playing first rather than lifting it.

RULE 23: LOOSE IMPEDIMENTS

One important point to commit firmly to memory is that sand and loose soil are loose impediments on the green, and may be brushed aside, but through the green they must not be touched. So there can be no pecking away at inconvenient accretions around your ball.

RULE 24: OBSTRUCTIONS

Being frail mortals we naturally feel miffed when we find the ball in a clearly unplayable spot, such as between two prominent tree roots. The first instinct is to cast around for a way of getting out of this predicament without paying a penalty. There is no casual water; it is not in ground under repair; but wait! This water pipe interferes with your intended swing. You inform your playing companion that you are entitled to relief from an immovable obstruction. He now has the exquisite pleasure of growling at you: 'No way, José'; and he is correct. Such relief is not permissible if a ball is clearly unplayable for any reason not connected with the obstruction. There is, however, a new rule (24-2c) which provides free relief for a ball lost in an immovable obstruction, instead of treating it under the regular provision for a lost ball.

RULE 25: ABNORMAL GROUND CONDITIONS

Here we have the intriguing situation of a rule saying one thing and an explanatory decision saying the opposite. Rule

25-2 permits a ball which is embedded in its own pitch mark to be lifted, cleaned and dropped without penalty *as near as possible to the spot where it lay*. The words 'as near as possible' admit of only one interpretation and that is back in the pitch mark. Yet Decision 25. (2) (3) states that a dropped ball which rolls back into its pitch mark may be re-dropped.

RULE 26: WATER HAZARDS

There is no penalty for replacing a ball lost in casual water. But it costs a penalty stroke to replace a ball lost in a water hazard. When a water hazard overflows its boundary, such overflow is casual water. What do you do if you cannot determine whether your ball is lost within the margin of the hazard or in the casual water area of this flood? Bite on the bullet and take relief under penalty.

RULE 28: BALL UNPLAYABLE

This rule is the golfer's friend because for once he is in control of his own destiny. He can declare his ball unplayable for any reason (unless it lies in a water hazard), or no reason except for an eccentric whim. It is comforting to have this privilege on call, especially when contemplating a high-risk shot. The player tells himself that if he gets into bad trouble he can always declare his ball unplayable.

If you leave the ball in a water hazard with your attempt to get out you can, exceptionally, play from the spot where you played the last stroke outside the hazard, under penalty of one stroke (Rule 26-2).

As for the remaining rules they concern different forms of golf, beset by pitfalls, disputes and appendices concerned with the technicalities of equipment. There is no need to master all this legislation, provided you carry a copy of the Rules in your golf bag for reference in times of doubt and distress. As for equipment and its specifications, you will not go wrong if you buy your clubs and balls from reputable manufacturers. In particular, do not dabble in the evil machinations of the legislation concerning the shape, dimension and spacing of grooves. That way madness lies.

THE STANDARD SCRATCH SCORE AND HANDICAPPING SCHEME

Implemented 1983, since revised

This scheme does not apply to ladies' clubs under the jurisdiction of the Ladies' Golf Union.

Published and administered by the Council of National Golf Unions and adopted by the Unions affiliated to the European Golf Association.

FOREWORD

The Standard Scratch Score and Handicapping Scheme was prepared by the British Golf Unions' Joint Advisory Council in 1925 at the request of the Royal & Ancient Golf Club of St Andrews and has been in operation throughout Great Britain and Ireland since 1 March, 1926.

The Scheme incorporated in this book, known as the Standard Scratch Score and Handicapping Scheme 1983, introduced a new concept in handicapping based on the system presently in use by the Australian Golf Union and which takes account of all scores returned by players under Medal Play conditions.

No change has been made in the present method of fixing the Standard Scratch Scores of courses but, on the principle that uniformity and equity in handicapping can be more effectively achieved if there is uniformity and equity in the fixing of Standard Scratch Scores, the Council of National Golf Unions has examined the Course Rating System of the United States Golf Association and has agreed that the Scratch Rating calculated by that procedure may be progressively adopted by National Unions as the Standard Scratch Score pursuant to clause 1.

Unions may now direct that the Standard Scratch Score be calculated in accordance with the Scratch Score Rating Procedure of the United States Golf Association.

Amended editions of this Scheme were published on 1 January 1966 and 1 January 1989. Further amendments since made are incorporated in this revised edition of the Scheme.

The principal changes are:

(a) The definition of a 'Member' in relation to the scheme (Definition E).
(b) The introduction of a different "Buffer Zone" depending on Categories of Handicap (Definition T and Clause 16).
(c) The restriction of allocating a Standard Scratch Score to courses measuring between 3000 and 4000 yards (Clause 1(6)).
(d) The use of the Scratch Score Rating Procedure of the United States Golf Association (Clause 1(7)).
(e) The permitted adjustment to a Measured Course to include

the use of a temporary tee (Clause 7(a)).

(f) The use of preferred lies is permitted between 1 October and 30 April (Clause 6).

(g) Unions are now required to establish a procedure to adjudicate upon Suspension of Handicaps (Clause 9(9)). This requirement imposes subsequent obligations on Area Authorities (Clause 10(3) and Affiliated Clubs (Clause 11(5)).

(h) Handicap Committees will in future report to Union and Area Authority reductions of members' playing handicaps to below scratch (Clause 12 (6)(d)).

(i) Alteration of Handicaps. With the introduction of different Buffer Zones there are adjustments to Procedure and Tables (Clause 16).

(j) Discretion is given to Unions to impose a maximum handicap increase under Clause 16(6) in a calendar year (Clause 16(10)(b)).

(k) Suspension, lapsing and loss of Handicaps. This clause has been amended (Clause 17).

(l) The procedure for Restoration of Handicaps following suspension, lapse or loss, has been changed (Clause 18).

(m) The Procedure & Tables for calculating the Competition Scratch Score (including the omission of Category 4 scores) have been altered.

(n) Handicap Allowances recommended by the Council of National Golf Unions (Appendix G).

(o) Decisions 1, 7 & 8 have been amended (Appendix I).

(p) Specific requirements relating to Computer Software (Appendix H).

PART ONE
DEFINITIONS

Definition

A UNION

B AREA AUTHORITY

C AFFILIATED CLUB

D HOME CLUB

E MEMBER

F HANDICAPPING AUTHORITY

G HANDICAP COMMITTEE

H HANDICAPS

I CATEGORIES OF HANDICAP

J MEASURED COURSE

K DISTANCE POINT

L MEDAL TEE

M MEDAL PLAY CONDITIONS

N QUALIFYING COMPETITION

O QUALIFYING SCORE

PART TWO
THE GOLF COURSE AND THE STANDARD SCRATCH SCORE

Clause

PART THREE
HANDICAPPING

PART ONE

DEFINITIONS

Throughout the Scheme whenever a word or expression is used which is defined within the following definitions the word or expression is printed in capital letters.

A – Union

A UNION is any national organisation in control of amateur golf in any country.

B – Area Authority

An AREA AUTHORITY is any authority appointed by a UNION to act on behalf of that UNION for the purposes of the Scheme within a specified area.

C – Affiliated Club

An AFFILIATED CLUB is a club affiliated to a UNION or AREA AUTHORITY which pays to the UNION and AREA AUTHORITY a specified annual per capita fee in respect of each eligible MEMBER.

D – Home Club

A player's HOME CLUB is an AFFILIATED CLUB of which the player is a MEMBER. If the player is a MEMBER of more than one AFFILIATED CLUB he shall nominate one as his HOME CLUB.

E – Member

A MEMBER is an amateur golfer who is eligible to compete in all QUALIFYING COMPETITIONS arranged by an AFFILIATED CLUB subject only to exclusion by virtue of one or more of the following:

(a) Restrictions imposed relating solely to the handicap of the players who may compete; or
(b) Restrictions imposed relating solely to the age of the players who may compete; or
(c) Such other restrictions as may be permitted by the UNION provided that any restrictions so permitted shall stipulate a minimum number of QUALIFYING

COMPETITIONS in a calendar year in which the MEMBER shall have a reasonable opportunity to compete.

Note: Under this definition a MEMBER need not necessarily be a member as defined by the constitution or rules of his AFFILIATED CLUB or CLUBS.

F – Handicapping Authority

The HANDICAPPING AUTHORITY for a player is his HOME CLUB subject to the overall jurisdiction of the UNION.

G – Handicap Committee

The HANDICAP COMMITTEE is the body appointed by an AFFILIATED CLUB to administer the Scheme within the CLUB.

H – Handicaps

(1) EXACT HANDICAP – a player's EXACT HANDICAP is his handicap calculated in accordance with the provisions of the Scheme to one decimal place.

(2) PLAYING HANDICAP – A PLAYER'S PLAYING HANDICAP is his EXACT HANDICAP calculated to the nearest whole number (0.5 is rounded upwards).

I – Categories of Handicap

Handicaps are divided into the following CATEGORIES :

CATEGORY 1: Handicaps of 5 or less.

CATEGORY 2: Handicaps of 6 to 12 inclusive.

CATEGORY 3: Handicaps of 13 to 20 inclusive.

CATEGORY 4: Handicaps of 21 to 28 inclusive.

J – Measured Course

Any course played over by an AFFILIATED CLUB the measured length of which has been certified in accordance with the requirements of clause 2.

K – Distance Point

The DISTANCE POINT is the position of a permanent marker indicating the point from which the length of a hole is measured.

L – Medal Tee

A MEDAL TEE is a rectangular area the front of which shall not be more than 10 yards (9 metres) in front of the relevant DISTANCE POINT and the rear of which shall not be less than 2 yards (2 metres) behind the DISTANCE POINT.

Note: Special rules apply when the length of a MEASURED COURSE has been temporarily reduced – see clause 7.

M – Medal Play Conditions

MEDAL PLAY CONDITIONS prevail during stroke, par and Stableford competitions played with full handicap allowance over 18 holes under the Rules of Golf from MEDAL TEES. MEDAL PLAY CONDITIONS shall not prevail when the length of the course played varies by more than 100 yards (91 metres) from the length of the MEASURED COURSE.

Note: Special rules apply when the length of a MEASURED COURSE has been temporarily reduced – see clause 7.

N – Qualifying Competition

A QUALIFYING COMPETITION is any competition in which MEDAL PLAY CONDITIONS prevail and for which a COMPETITION SCRATCH SCORE is calculated subject to restrictions and limitations contained in the Scheme or imposed by UNIONS.

O – Qualifying Score

A QUALIFYING SCORE is any score including a 'no return' returned in a QUALIFYING COMPETITION.

P – Aggregate Four-ball Competition

An AGGREGATE FOUR-BALL COMPETITION is a QUALIFYING COMPETITION in which the completed scores at each hole of a team of not more than two amateur players are aggregated.

Q – Standard Scratch Score

The STANDARD SCRATCH SCORE is the score allotted to an 18 hole golf course after the application of clause 1.

R – Competition Scratch Score

The COMPETITION SCRATCH SCORE is the score determined by clause 20.

S – Nett Differential

The NETT DIFFERENTIAL is the difference (+ or -) between the nett score returned by a player in a QUALIFYING COMPETITION and the COMPETITION SCRATCH SCORE.

T – Buffer Zone

A score is within a player's BUFFER ZONE when a NETT DIFFERENTIAL is within the following bands for his HANDICAP CATEGORY.

CATEGORY 1 0 to +1
CATEGORY 2 0 to +2
CATEFORY 3 0 to +3
CATEGORY 4 0 to +4

Note: When a player's score is within his BUFFER ZONE his EXACT HANDICAP remains unchanged.

PART TWO

THE GOLF COURSE AND THE STANDARD SCRATCH SCORE

1. The Standard Scratch Score

1.(1) The STANDARD SCRATCH SCORE is the score which a scratch player is expected to return in ideal conditions over a MEASURED COURSE. In the case of a nine-hole course it represents two rounds.

1.(2) The allocation of STANDARD SCRATCH SCORES shall be the responsibility of the UNION.

1.(3) The Table below will provide a guide to officials in making their assessments.

1.(4) In assessing the STANDARD SCRATCH SCORE of a course, officials will take as the starting point the Provisional Standard Scratch Score from the Table. They will then consider the following points:

TABLE OF PROVISIONAL STANDARD SCRATCH SCORES

Standard length of Course	Lengths included in Standard Length		Provisional Standard Scratch Score
Yards	Yards	Metres	
7100	7001-7200	6402-6584	74
6900	6801-7000	6219-6401	73
6700	6601-6800	6036-6218	72
6500	6401-6600	5853-6035	71
6300	6201-6400	5670-5852	70
6100	5951-6200	5442-5669	69
5800	5701-5950	5213-5441	68
5500	5451-5700	4984-5212	67
5300	5201-5450	4756-4983	66
5100	5001-5200	4573-4755	65
4900	4801-5000	4390-4572	64
4700	4601-4800	4207-4389	63
4500	4401-4600	4024-4206	62
4300	4201-4400	3841-4023	61
4100	4001-4200	3659-3840	60

1 yard = 0.91440 metres 1 metre = 1.09361 yards

(a) The terrain and general layout of the course.

(b) Normal ground conditions – Is run average, above average or below average?

(c) Sizes of greens and whether watered or unwatered.

(d) Hazards – Are greens well guarded or open?

(e) Width of fairways, the effect of trees and nature of rough.

(f) Nearness of 'out of bounds' to fairways and greens.

(g) Average weather conditions throughout the playing year. Is the course exposed and subject to high winds for most of the year? Is it sheltered from the full effects of adverse weather?

(h) The distance by which the length of the course varies from the standard length shown in column one of the Table.

1.(5) Having considered all these points, officials will fix the STANDARD SCRATCH SCORE of the course by:

(a) Confirming the Provisional Standard Scratch Score as the STANDARD SCRATCH SCORE.

(b) Adding a stroke or strokes to the Provisional Standard Scratch Score.

(c) Deducting a stroke or strokes from the Provisional Standard Scratch Score.

1.(6) With effect from 1 January 1993 no course of less than 3,000 yards shall be allocated a STANDARD SCRATCH SCORE. At the discretion of a UNION courses between 3,000 and 4,000 yards may be allocated such STANDARD SCRATCH SCORE as the UNION shall determine.

1.(7) A UNION may direct that the STANDARD SCRATCH SCORE shall be in accordance with the Scratch Score Rating Procedure of The United States Golf Association.

2. Course Measurement

Measurement shall be by plan or projection along the horizontal plane from the DISTANCE POINT on the MEDAL TEE to the centre of the green of each hole.

In the case of a dog-leg hole, measurement shall be along the centre line of the fairway to the axis and then to the centre of the green. Measurement shall be carried out by a qualified surveyor, or someone competent and experienced in the handling of surveying instruments, who shall grant a certificate showing details of the length of each hole and the total playing length of the course. Subsequent alterations to the length of the course will require a certificate only for the altered hole or holes which shall be measured in the manner prescribed above.

3. Alterations to Courses

When alterations have been carried out to a course increasing or decreasing its length, the club shall submit a 'Form of Application' through its AREA AUTHORITY to the UNION. In the case of a new course, a 'Form of Application' shall be submitted by the club through its AREA AUTHORITY to the UNION who will fix the STANDARD SCRATCH SCORE. The UNION is responsible for all STANDARD SCRATCH SCORES in the country over which it has jurisdiction.

4. Tees

All clubs with the requisite facilities should have back and forward MEDAL TEES with a yardage measurement from each tee and a separate STANDARD SCRATCH SCORE as measured from back and forward MEDAL TEES permanently marked.

Wherever possible when courses are being remeasured the DISTANCE POINT on each MEDAL TEE should be so positioned that the tee markers when placed adjacent to the DISTANCE POINT provide a teeing area which satisfies the following recommendation of the Royal & Ancient Golf Club of St Andrews:

'Committees should bear in mind the definition of "Teeing Ground" (Rules of Golf) which states: "It is a rectangular area two club-lengths in depth". The Tee Markers should be placed in such a position that the player has the benefit of the full depth to which the definition entitles him'.

To facilitate the use of the correct tees the Royal & Ancient Golf Club of St Andrews recommends that tee boxes or other objects in use to mark the teeing ground shall be painted as follows:

Ladies' Standard MEDAL TEES	Red
Men's Forward MEDAL TEES	Yellow
Men's Back MEDAL TEES	White

When a National Championship is being played over a course the tee markers may be coloured Blue.

5. Par

The STANDARD SCRATCH SCORE must not be allocated amongst the individual holes, but should be printed as a total on the card. The par figure for each hole should be printed alongside each hole on the card. Par for each hole shall be fixed by the club in relation to the length and playing difficulty of each hole and shall be fixed within the following ranges:

	Yards	*Metres*
Par 3	0-250	0-229
Par 4	220-500	201-457
Par 5	440+	402+

eg if a hole is 460 yards (421 metres) it may be allotted par 4 or 5 depending upon its average playing difficulty.

The total of the par figures for each hole of a course will not necessarily coincide with the STANDARD SCRATCH SCORE of that course. Par figures should be used for Stableford, Par, and similar competitions.

6. Preferred Lies

When preferred lies are in operation the following points shall be taken into consideration: MEDAL PLAY CONDITIONS will apply notwithstanding the application of a Local Rule for preferred lies as a result of adverse conditions during the period from 1 October to 30 April. Preferred lies may be used during that period but are not mandatory upon clubs during any part thereof. The Local Rule may apply to specified holes only. Outside that period MEDAL PLAY CONDITIONS will not apply if preferred lies are in operation unless the consent of the UNION or AREA AUTHORITY has been first obtained.

It is emphasised that preferred lies shall apply only when a Local Rule has been made and published in accordance with Appendix 1 of the Rules of Golf as follows:

'A ball lying on any "closely mown area" through the green may, without penalty, be moved or may be lifted, cleaned and placed within six inches of where it originally lay, but not nearer the hole. After the ball has been so moved or placed, it is in play.'

Penalty for breach of Local Rule: Match-Play – Loss of hole; Stroke-play – Two strokes.

Note: 'closely mown area' means any area of the course, including paths through the rough, cut to fairway height or less. (Rule 25-2).

7. Permitted Adjustment to a Measured Course

Whilst each AFFILIATED CLUB must endeavour to maintain the length of its MEASURED COURSE at all times MEDAL PLAY CONDITIONS nevertheless prevail when the length of a course has been reduced in the following circumstances:

(a) When, to allow movement of the playing position on the MEDAL TEE or the use of a temporary green or tee, the length of the course being played has been reduced by not more than 100 yards (91· metres) from the length of the MEASURED COURSE.

(b) When, to allow work to proceed on course alterations or for reasons other than weather conditions, it is necessary to reduce the playing length of the MEASURED COURSE by between 100 and 300 yards (91 and 274 metres). In these circumstances, the club shall reduce the STANDARD SCRATCH SCORE of the MEASURED COURSE temporarily by 1 stroke and report to the UNION, or to such other body nominated by the UNION, the reduction in the STANDARD SCRATCH SCORE, and the reason for it. The club must also notify the UNION or other body when the course has been restored to its measured length and the official STANDARD SCRATCH SCORE reinstated.

PART THREE

HANDICAPPING

8. Introduction

8.(1) The Council of National Golf Unions Standard Scratch Score and Handicapping Scheme has been revised to achieve a uniformity and equity in handicapping throughout Great Britain and Ireland and those member countries of the European Golf Association adopting the Scheme. The nature of the game of golf, with its varying playing conditions, makes handicapping a relatively inexact operation. Nevertheless, if the same principles are sensibly and universally applied by HANDICAP COMMITTEES, a high degree of uniformity in handicapping can be achieved. It is therefore of paramount importance that all parties to the Scheme fulfil their obligations to it and these are set out below.

8.(2) Handicapping within the Scheme is delegated to AFFILIATED CLUBS subject to the overall jurisdiction of the UNION.

9. Rights and Obligations of the Union

The UNION:

9.(1) Shall have overall jurisdiction for the administration of the Scheme.

9.(2) May delegate any part of that jurisdiction to an AREA AUTHORITY.

9.(3) Shall ratify all PLAYING HANDICAPS reduced to below scratch on the first occasion in any calendar year, immediately after the reduction.

9.(4) Shall have the right to obtain information upon handicaps from AFFILIATED CLUBS at any time.

9.(5) Shall establish within the UNION conditions, restrictions and limitations to be imposed in respect of competitions deemed to be QUALIFYING COMPETITIONS.

9.(6) Shall settle any dispute referred to it. Its decision shall be final.

9.(7) May at its discretion authorise HOME CLUBS to increase the handicaps of players in any of the CATEGORIES 2, 3, and 4 pursuant to clause 19. When such authority has been given the requirement of clause 19.(2) and (3) that the increase shall be effected by the UNION or AREA AUTHORITY shall not apply. Notwithstanding the foregoing, the UNION may, if it considers that handicaps have been unjustifiably increased by a HOME CLUB, require that club to comply with all of the provisions of clause 19.

9.(8) May at its discretion direct that scores returned by a player in CATEGORIES 3 and/or 4 at a club which is not his HOME CLUB or alternatively at a club of which he is not a MEMBER shall be disregarded for handicap increase pursuant to clause 16.(3).

9.(9) Establish a procedure to adjudicate upon the suspension of handicaps pursuant to clause 17(1) and appoint a committee to perform duties referred to in that clause.

10. Rights and Obligations of the Area Authority

The AREA AUTHORITY shall:

10.(1) Administer the responsibilities delegated to it by the UNION.

10.(2) Have the right to obtain information upon handicaps from AFFILIATED CLUBS at any time.

10.(3) Appoint a committee to perform the duties referred to in clause 17(1).

11. Rights and Obligations of the Affiliated Club

The AFFILIATED CLUB shall:

11.(1) Act as the HANDICAPPING AUTHORITY for all members for whom it is the HOME CLUB subject to the overall jurisdiction of the UNION.

11.(2) Ensure that the Scheme is properly applied in the club.

11.(3) Ensure that with effect from 1 January 1994 any computer software used for the calculation of handicaps shall satisfy the requirements set out in Appendix H.

11.(4) Ensure that all handicaps are calculated in accordance with the Scheme.

11.(5) Appoint a HANDICAP COMMITTEE of which the majority shall be MEMBERS to perform the obligations set out in clause 12 below.

11.(6) Appoint a committee of which the majority shall be MEMBERS to perform the duties referred to in clause 17(1).

12. Rights and Obligations of the Handicap Committee

The HANDICAP COMMITTEE shall:

12.(1) Maintain a list in which the names of competitors must be entered prior to competing in a QUALIFYING COMPETITION at the club.

12.(2) Ensure, so far as possible, that all cards taken out in QUALIFYING COMPETITIONS are returned to the committee including incomplete cards.

12.(3) At the conclusion of each round of a QUALIFYING COMPETITION calculate the COMPETITION SCRATCH SCORE as required by clause 20.

12.(4) Post on the club's notice board all changes of MEMBERS' PLAYING HANDICAPS immediately they are made.

12.(5) Ensure that a record of MEMBERS' current PLAYING HANDICAPS is available in a prominent position in the clubhouse.

12.(6) When the club is a player's HOME CLUB:

(a) Maintain on his behalf a handicap record sheet which shall include all the information shown in Appendix A.

(b) Ensure his scores are recorded immediately after completion of each QUALIFYING COMPETITION at the HOME CLUB or the reporting of a QUALIFYING SCORE returned elsewhere, and that all EXACT HANDICAPS are calculated in relation to scores recorded in chronological order.

(c) Keep his EXACT HANDICAP up to date at all times.

(d) Notify the UNION and AREA AUTHORITY immediately the committee reduces a MEMBER'S PLAYING HANDICAP to below scratch on the first occasion in any calendar year and obtain ratification from the UNION, or, if so delegated, from the AREA AUTHORITY.

Note: The reduction is effective before ratification.

(e) Unless some other body has been appointed by the HOME CLUB for this purpose, exercise the power to suspend handicaps contained in clause 17.

(f) When a MEMBER changes his HOME CLUB send to the new HOME CLUB a copy of the player's current handicap record sheet.

(g) Specify the conditions which apply when a player wishes to obtain a handicap under the provisions of clause 15.

(h) Exercise the powers to adjust players' handicaps contained in clause 19.

(i) As required by clause 19.(5) advise players of changes made to their handicaps under the provisions of clause 19.

13. Rights and Obligations of the Player

The player shall:

13.(1) Have one handicap only which shall be allotted and adjusted by his HOME CLUB. That handicap shall apply elsewhere including other clubs of which the player is a MEMBER.

13.(2) If he is a MEMBER of more than one AFFILIATED CLUB select one as his HOME CLUB and notify that club and the others of his choice.

13.(3) Not change his HOME CLUB except by giving advance notice of the change which can take effect only at the end of a calendar year unless he has ceased to be a member of his HOME CLUB or both clubs agree to the change taking place at an earlier date.

13.(4) Report to his HOME CLUB the names of all other AFFILIATED CLUBS of which he is, becomes, or ceases to be, a MEMBER and report to all other AFFILIATED CLUBS of which he is a MEMBER:

(a) The name of his HOME CLUB and any changes of his HOME CLUB and

(b) Alterations to his PLAYING HANDICAP made by his HOME CLUB.

13.(5) Ensure that before competing in a QUALIFYING COMPETITION his entry has been inserted in the competition entry list.

13.(6) Ensure that all competition cards in QUALIFYING COMPETITIONS, whether or not complete, are returned to the organising committee.

13.(7) Subject to the provisions of clause 9.(8) report to his HOME CLUB immediately all QUALIFYING SCORES (including no returns) returned away from his HOME CLUB advising the HOME CLUB of the date of the QUALIFYING COMPETITION, the venue and the COMPETITION SCRATCH SCORE together with the following:

(a) After a stroke-play QUALIFYING COMPETITION the gross score returned.

(b) After a Stableford QUALIFYING COMPETITION the par of the course and the number of points scored.

(c) After a par QUALIFYING COMPETITION the par of the course and the score versus par.

Note 1: Players are reminded that failure to report scores returned away from their HOME CLUBS (including no returns) when so required by the scheme is likely to lead to the suspension of offending players' handicaps under the provisions of clause 17.

Note 2: In the event of a QUALIFYING COMPETITION being declared abandoned or scores returned being deemed by clause 20 not to be QUALIFYING SCORES the player is required to report the above information only if he has returned a NETT DIFFERENTIAL of less than zero.

13.(8) Prior to playing in any competition at a club other than his HOME CLUB ensure that any appropriate reductions to his PLAYING HANDICAP have been made or alternatively comply with the obligations set out in clause 16.(11).

13.(9) Enter his current PLAYING HANDICAP on all cards returned in a QUALIFYING COMPETITION even though the event may not be a handicap competition.

13.(10) Provide to his HOME CLUB such information regarding scores in non-qualifying competitions if so directed by a UNION.

14. Qualifying Scores

14.(1) The only scores to be recorded on a player's handicap record sheet are:

(a) QUALIFYING SCORES as defined.

(b) NETT DIFFERENTIALS of less than zero returned in any abandoned round of a QUALIFYING COMPETITION or in any round of a QUALIFYING COMPETITION when that round has been deemed under the provisions of clause 20 not to be a QUALIFYING SCORE.

(c) Correct scores in a QUALIFYING COMPETITION which are disqualified for any reason.

(d) Scores returned in a QUALIFYING COMPETITION played over 18 holes on a course reduced in length under the provisions of clause 7.

(e) Scores returned in a QUALIFYING COMPETITION played over a MEASURED COURSE when Local Rules are in operation for preferred lies (as permitted by clause 6) or for any other purpose provided the rules are authorised by Appendix 1 of the Rules of Golf or associated guidance notes or have been approved by the Rules of Golf Committee of the Royal & Ancient Golf Club of St Andrews.

(f)   The individual scores and no returns returned by players in AGGREGATE FOUR-BALL COMPETITIONS.

Note 1: The competition must be a QUALIFYING COMPETITION.

Note 2: QUALIFYING SCORES returned in Stableford and par competitions shall be converted into NETT DIFFERENTIALS by using the tables in Appendix C.

14.(2) The following returns shall not be accepted as QUALIFYING SCORES in any circumstances:

(a) Scores returned in any better ball four-ball competition.

(b) Scores returned in competitions over less than 18 holes.

(c) Scores returned in any competition which is not played in accordance with the Rules of Golf and authorised Local Rules eg a competition which limits the number of clubs permitted to less than 14.

(c) Scores returned in an extended competition in which the player has the option of selecting the day or days on which he shall compete and/or how many returns he shall make except the following competitions in which only one return is permitted:

(i) A competition over no more than two days which need not be consecutive, or

(ii) A competition extended over three or more days solely to accommodate the number of players entered.

(e) Subject to clause 14.(1)(b) scores returned in any round of a QUALIFYING COMPETITION deemed under the provisions of clause 20 not to be QUALIFYING SCORES.

(f)   Any competition other than an AGGREGATE FOUR-BALL COMPETITION in which competitors play in partnership with another competitor.

(g) Stableford and par competitions played with less than full handicap allowance.

(h) Scores returned in events run by organisations which are not HANDICAPPING AUTHORITIES unless such events have been previously approved by a UNION as a QUALIFYING COMPETITION.

15. Allotment of Handicaps

15.(1) The maximum handicap is 28. (Maximum EXACT HANDICAP 28.0.)

15.(2) A handicap can be allotted only to a MEMBER of an AFFILIATED CLUB.

15.(3) To obtain a handicap a player shall submit three cards preferably marked over a MEASURED COURSE which shall be adjusted by the HANDICAP COMMITTEE so that any score of more than 2 over par at any hole shall be amended to 2 over par. After these adjustments have been made an EXACT HANDICAP shall be allotted equivalent to the number of strokes by which the best of the three rounds differs from the STANDARD SCRATCH SCORE. The HANDICAP COMMITTEE may allot a player an initial whole number EXACT HANDICAP less than the best score if it has reason to consider that a lower handicap is more appropriate to the player's ability. In exceptional circumstances a higher handicap may be allotted than that indicated by the best score.

When a player fails to return cards justifying an EXACT HANDICAP of 28.0 he may, at the discretion of the HANDICAP COMMITTEE, be given an EXACT HANDICAP of 28.0. The player's PLAYING HANDICAP shall equal the EXACT HANDICAP allotted. AFFILIATED CLUBS may at their absolute discretion refuse to allot a handicap until a specified standard has been attained.

15.(4) A player without a handicap shall not be allotted a CATEGORY 1 HANDICAP without the written authority of the UNION, or AREA AUTHORITY if so delegated.

16. Alteration of Handicaps

16.(1) Definition I divides handicaps into the following four CATEGORIES:

CATEGORY 1: Handicaps of 5 or less.

CATEGORY 2: Handicaps of 6 to 12 inclusive.

CATEGORY 3: Handicaps of 13 to 20 inclusive.

CATEGORY 4: Handicaps of 21 to 28 inclusive.

16.(2) If a player returns a NETT DIFFERENTIAL within his BUFFER ZONE his EXACT HANDICAP is not changed.

16.(3) Subject to the provisions of clauses 9.(8), 20.(3) and 20.(4), if a player returns a score with a NETT DIFFEREN-TIAL above his BUFFER ZONE or records a "no return" his EXACT HANDICAP is increased by 0.1.

16.(4) If a player returns a NETT DIFFERENTIAL of less than zero his EXACT HANDICAP is reduced by an amount *per stroke that the* NETT DIFFERENTIAL *is below zero*, the amount per stroke being determined by his HANDICAP CATEGORY.

16.(5) The recording of scores shall be kept by NETT DIF-FERENTIAL ie the difference (+ or -) between the player's nett score and the COMPETITION SCRATCH SCORE. The date, NETT DIFFERENTIAL, EXACT HANDICAP and PLAYING HANDICAP must be recorded on the player's handicap record sheet.

16.(6) EXACT HANDICAPS shall be adjusted as follows, with reference to the handicap adjustment table, Appendix B opposite.

For example:

If a player on 11.2 returns a score with a NETT DIFFER-ENTIAL of 4 his EXACT HANDICAP becomes 11.3. If he then returns a score with a NETT DIFFERENTIAL of -7 his EXACT HANDICAP is reduced by 7 times 0.2 = 1.4, ie to an EXACT HANDICAP of 9.9 and his PLAYING HANDICAP is 10 which is immediately his new handicap.

APPENDIX B: HANDICAP ADJUSTMENT TABLE

CATEGORY	PLAYING HANDICAP	If NETT DIFFERENTIAL is:	
		Above BUFFER ZONE. Add *only*	Below CSS. SUBTRACT for *each* Stroke below
1	Up to 5	0.1	0.1
2	6 to 12	0.1	0.2
3	13 to 20	0.1	0.3
4	21 to 28	0.1	0.4

16.(7) When a player's handicap is to be reduced so that it goes from a higher CATEGORY to a lower CATEGORY, it shall be reduced at the rate appropriate to the higher CATEGORY only so far as brings his PLAYING HANDICAP into the lower CATEGORY and the balance of the reduction shall be at the rate appropriate to the lower CATEGORY.

For example:

If a player on 21.2 returns a score with a NETT DIFFERENTIAL of -6, ie 6 strokes below his PLAYING HANDICAP of 21, his handicap is reduced as follows:

21.2-(2 times 0.4) (ie -8)=20.4
20.4-(4 times 0.3) (ie -1.2)=19.2

16.(8) A player whose EXACT HANDICAP contains 0.5 or over shall be given the next higher handicap, eg 12.5 exact would be 13 PLAYING HANDICAP. This applies when handicaps are to be increased or reduced.

Note: EXACT HANDICAP -0.5 rounded upwards is PLAYING HANDICAP scratch and not plus one.

16.(9) Reductions of PLAYING HANDICAPS shall be made on the day the score becomes known to the HOME CLUB.

16.(10)

(a) Increases of PLAYING HANDICAPS shall be made at the end of each calendar month or at such shorter intervals as the HOME CLUB may decide.

(b) A UNION may at its discretion restrict an increase of EXACT HANDICAPS to 2.0 strokes in a calendar year except increases granted under clause 19.

16.(11) If, for any reason, a player is unable to report to his HOME CLUB a QUALIFYING SCORE or SCORES which may have a NETT DIFFERENTIAL of less than zero or has been unable to ascertain, after reporting such scores, whether or not his PLAYING HANDICAP has been reduced, he shall then, before competing in a further competition at a club other than his HOME CLUB, either:

(a) For that competition only, make such reduction to his PLAYING HANDICAP as shall be appropriate under the Scheme by applying the COMPETITION SCRATCH SCORE if known, otherwise the STANDARD SCRATCH SCORE to his gross score, or

(b) Report to the committee organising the competition any relevant score returned which after deduction of his PLAYING HANDICAP is two above the STANDARD SCRATCH SCORE or less. The committee may, for that competition only, reduce the player's PLAYING HANDICAP.

Note: Increases to PLAYING HANDICAPS may not be made under the provisions of this sub clause.

16.(12) The procedure for the restoration of handicaps which have been lost is contained in clause 18.

17. Suspension, Lapsing and Loss of Handicaps

17.(1) Subject to the provisions of Clause 17(2) the UNION, AREA AUTHORITY or a player's HOME CLUB shall suspend the handicap of any player who in its opinion has:

(a) Constantly or blatantly failed to comply with the obligations and responsibilities imposed by this Scheme, or

(b) Conducted himself in a manner prejudicial to the interests of his UNION, AREA AUTHORITY or HOME CLUB or to the game of Golf.

The player must be notified of the period of suspension and of any other conditions imposed. No player's handicap shall be suspended without first affording him the opportunity of appearing before the committee or other body.

17.(2) Subject to any directions to the contrary issued by a UNION no proceedings pursuant to Clause 17(1) shall be considered by an AREA AUTHORITY or HOME CLUB without the written authority of the UNION. Following the receipt of a request for such an authority, UNIONS shall direct whether the UNION, the AREA AUTHORITY or HOME CLUB shall hear and determine the issue. UNIONS shall direct the appeal procedure to be made available to a player should be he dissatisfied with the determination. Subject to any directions made by a UNION this restriction shall not apply to proceedings brought against a MEMBER by his HOME CLUB in respect of an alleged offence committed at that club.

17.(3) If a player is suspended from membership of his HOME CLUB his handicap shall lapse automatically until his membership is reinstated.

17.(4) A player's handicap is lost immediately he ceases to be a MEMBER of an AFFILIATED CLUB or loses his amateur status.

17.(5) Whilst a player's handicap is suspended, lapsed or has been lost he shall not enter or compete in any competition which requires a competitor to be the holder of a CONGU handicap as designated by this scheme for either entering or competing in the competition.

17.(6) The suspension of a player's handicap shall apply at all AFFILIATED CLUBS of which the player is or becomes a MEMBER during the period of suspension.

18. Restoration of Handicaps

18.(1) If the handicap of a player is to be reinstated within 6 months of the date on which his handicap was lost, or suspended or lapsed upon his suspension from membership of his HOME CLUB it shall be reinstated at the same handicap the player last held. In all other cases the player shall be allotted a new handicap after he has complied with the requirements of Clause 15.

18.(2) When allotting a new handicap to a player the HANDICAP COMMITTEE shall give due consideration to the handicap he last held and a CATEGORY 1 HANDICAP shall not be allotted without the written approval of the UNION or AREA AUTHORITY if so delegated.

19. Powers of the Handicap Committee Relating to General Play

19.(1) Whenever the HANDICAP COMMITTEE of a player's HOME CLUB considers that a player's EXACT HANDICAP is too high and does no reflect his current playing ability the HANDICAP COMMITTEE must, subject to the provisions of sub clause (3) of this clause, reduce his EXACT HANDICAP to the figure it considers appropriate.

19.(2)

(a) Whenever the HANDICAP COMMITTEE of a player's HOME CLUB considers that a player's EXACT HANDICAP is too low and does not reflect his current playing ability the HANDICAP COMMITTEE must, subject to the provisions of sub clause (3) of this clause, recommend to the UNION, or AREA AUTHORITY if so delegated, that his EXACT HANDICAP should be increased to the figure it considers appropriate.

(b) In the event of a UNION delegating to HOME CLUBS the unconditional authority to increase the handicaps of players in any of the CATEGORIES 2, 3 and 4 HOME CLUBS need not submit to the UNION or AREA AUTHORITY proposals in respect of any changes of handicaps of players in the nominated CATEGORIES.

19.(3) When the HANDICAP COMMITTEE has decided

(a) That the EXACT HANDICAP of a CATEGORY 1 player shall be reduced, or

(b) That the EXACT HANDICAP of a CATEGORY 2 player shall be reduced into CATEGORY 1, or

(c) That the EXACT HANDICAP of any player shall be increased (Subject to the provision of clause 9(7)).

Then the HANDICAP COMMITTEE must refer the matter to the UNION, or AREA AUTHORITY if so delegated, with its recommended adjustment. The UNION or AREA AUTHORITY shall then authorise the recommended variation, reject the recommendation or refer the matter back to the HANDICAP COMMITTEE for further consideration. The UNION or AREA AUTHORITY shall be supplied with all the information upon which the recommendation is based and with any further information required.

19.(4) When deciding whether to effect or recommend an adjustment of handicap the HANDICAP COMMITTEE of the player's HOME CLUB shall consider all available information regarding the player's golfing ability.

It shall consider in particular:

(a) The frequency of QUALIFYING SCORES recently returned by the player to and below his PLAYING HANDICAP.

(b) The player's achievement in match-play, four-ball better-ball competitions and other non-qualifying events.

(c) QUALIFYING SCORES returned by the player in stroke-play competitions which are adversely affected by one or more particularly bad holes. It may prove helpful to take into account the number of points the player would have scored if these QUALIFYING SCORES had been in Stableford competitions played with full handicap allowance.

19.(5) The HANDICAP COMMITTEE shall advise a player of any change of handicap under this clause and the change will become effective when the player becomes aware of the adjustment.

19.(6) The HANDICAP COMMITTEE or other body organising a competition at a club which is not the player's HOME CLUB may, if it considers that his handicap is too high because of scores reported pursuant to sub clause 16.(11)(b) or for any other reason, reduce that handicap. Any reduction made under this clause shall apply only to the competition for which it is made.

19.(7) An AFFILIATED CLUB may not apply a formula by which handicaps shall be adjusted under this clause. Any handicap so adjusted shall not be a CONGU handicap designated under this scheme.

19.(8) Decisions made by a HANDICAP COMMITTEE, UNION or AREA AUTHORITY under this clause shall be final.

Note 1: In the interests of equitable handicapping it is essential that all HANDICAP COMMITTEES keep the handicaps of the MEMBERS for whom they act as the HOME CLUB under review and that adjustments of handicaps are considered as soon as it comes to the committee's notice that a player's handicap may no longer correctly reflect his current general golfing ability.

Note 2: The HANDICAP COMMITTEE should consider dealing more severely with a player whose general standard of play is known to be improving than it should with a player who it is believed has returned scores below his general ability but whose general playing ability is not considered to be improving.

20. Competition Scratch Score

20.(1) At the conclusion of each round of a QUALIFYING COMPETITION the COMPETITION SCRATCH SCORE shall be calculated by following the procedure set out in Appendix D and applying the relevant Table in either Appendix E or F.

20.(2) In the event of one round of a QUALIFYING COMPETITION extending over more than one day the COMPETITION SCRATCH SCORE shall be calculated for each day.

20.(3) The relevant Table dictates any adjustment to be

made to the STANDARD SCRATCH SCORE to provide the COMPETITION SCRATCH SCORE or to direct that the scores returned shall not count as QUALIFYING SCORES (indicated by 'N/C' in the Table column heading). When the COMPETITION SCRATCH SCORE has been established all NETT DIFFERENTIALS shall be calculated in relation thereto and handicap adjustment made and entered in the player's Handicap Record Sheets. (See Definition T - BUFFER ZONE.)

20.(4) If the Table indicates that the scores returned shall not count as QUALIFYING SCORES then the COMPETITION SCRATCH SCORE shall be deemed to be three strokes more than the STANDARD SCRATCH SCORE. All players who after the application of the COMPETITION SCRATCH SCORE to their scores have returned a NETT DIFFERENTIAL of less than zero shall have their EXACT HANDICAPS reduced to the extent dictated by the NETT DIFFERENTIAL so calculated. A NETT DIFFERENTIAL or zero or above shall not result in a handicap increase.

20.(5) If a QUALIFYING COMPETITION is abandoned for any reason the COMPETITION SCRATCH SCORE shall be regarded as equal to the STANDARD SCRATCH SCORE and players returning NETT DIFFERENTIALS of less than zero shall have their EXACT HANDICAPS reduced to the extent dictated by the NETT DIFFERENTIAL. A NETT DIFFERENTIAL of zero or above shall not result in a handicap increase.

Note: UNIONS, AREA AUTHORITIES and any organisations so authorised by a UNION shall establish the COMPETITION SCRATCH SCORES for events they organise.

20.(6) Where a player is a MEMBER of two or more AFFILIATED CLUBS and competes in a QUALIFYING COMPETITION organised by two or more of those clubs and played over the same course and the score in one round is used in all the competitions then the COMPETITION SCRATCH SCORE applicable shall be that applied by his HOME CLUB or if none of the clubs is his HOME CLUB the highest COMPETITION SCRATCH SCORE shall be applied.

Appendix A
Handicap Record Sheet

NAME _____

HOME CLUB _____

OTHER CLUBS _____

Date	Nett differential	Handicap Exact	Playing	Date	Nett differential	Handicap Exact	Playing
May					June		
1	B/F	21.0	21	30	B/F	19.4	19
6	4	21.0	21	July			
7	5	21.0	21	8 (am)	7	19.5	19
20	N/R	21.2	21	8 (pm)	6	19.6	19
21	-6	19.2	19	29	8	19.7	19 [Note 2]
				30	4	19.8	20
June					Aug		
4	1	19.2	19	6	2	19.8	20
5	4	19.3	19	7	-6	18.0	18
25	7	19.4	19	20	0	18.0	18
26	2	19.4	19	21	7	18.1	18

NOTES TO APPENDIX A

1 The sheet above shows the PLAYING HANDICAPS when increases are made on the last day of each calendar month.

2 If the increases had been made immediately the PLAYING HANDICAP would have been increased to 20 on 8 July am and the NETT DIFFERENTIALS of 6, 8 and 4 respectively on 8 July pm, 29 and 30 July would each have been reduced by 1. Thus, with the operation of the BUFFER ZONE, the EXACT HANDICAP would have remained at 19.7 on 31 July and been 0.1 less than those shown thereafter.

3 NETT DIFFERENTIAL is the difference (+ or -) between the Nett Score returned by a player in a QUALIFYING COMPETITION and the COMPETITION SCRATCH SCORE.

4 Scores returned on courses other than that of the player's HOME CLUB should be distinguished by marking the NETT DIFFERENTIAL thus: '☐

5 Reductions of PLAYING HANDICAPS are effected immediately.

6 Increases of PLAYING HANDICAPS shall be made at the end of each calendar month or at such shorter intervals as the HOME CLUB may decide.

7 When scores are received by the HOME CLUB out of chronological order the player's EXACT HANDICAP shall be recorded so that it relates to chronological order.

Appendix B
Table of Handicap Adjustments

Nett Differentials	-1	-2	-3	-4	-5	-6	-7	-8	-9	-10	-11	-12	Over Buffer Zone
Exact Handicaps													
Up to 5.4	-0.1	-0.2	-0.3	-0.4	-0.5	-0.6	-0.7	-0.8	-0.9	-1.0	-1.1	-1.2	+0.1
5.5–5.6	-0.2	-0.3	-0.4	-0.5	-0.6	-0.7	-0.8	-0.9	-1.0	-1.1	-1.2	-1.3	+0.1
5.7–5.8	-0.2	-0.4	-0.5	-0.6	-0.7	-0.8	-0.9	-1.0	-1.1	-1.2	-1.3	-1.4	+0.1
5.9–6.0	-0.2	-0.4	-0.6	-0.7	-0.8	-0.9	-1.0	-1.1	-1.2	-1.3	-1.4	-1.5	+0.1
6.1–6.2	-0.2	-0.4	-0.6	-0.8	-0.9	-1.0	-1.1	-1.2	-1.3	-1.4	-1.5	-1.6	+0.1
6.3–6.4	-0.2	-0.4	-0.6	-0.8	-1.0	-1.1	-1.2	-1.3	-1.4	-1.5	-1.6	-1.7	+0.1
6.5–6.6	-0.2	-0.4	-0.6	-0.8	-1.0	-1.2	-1.3	-1.4	-1.5	-1.6	-1.7	-1.8	+0.1
6.7–6.8	-0.2	-0.4	-0.6	-0.8	-1.0	-1.2	-1.4	-1.5	-1.6	-1.7	-1.8	-1.9	+0.1
6.9–7.0	-0.2	-0.4	-0.6	-0.8	-1.0	-1.2	-1.4	-1.6	-1.7	-1.8	-1.9	-2.0	+0.1
7.1–7.2	-0.2	-0.4	-0.6	-0.8	-1.0	-1.2	-1.4	-1.6	-1.8	-1.9	-2.0	-2.1	+0.1
7.3–7.4	-0.2	-0.4	-0.6	-0.8	-1.0	-1.2	-1.4	-1.6	-1.8	-2.0	-2.1	-2.2	+0.1
7.5–7.6	-0.2	-0.4	-0.6	-0.8	-1.0	-1.2	-1.4	-1.6	-1.8	-2.0	-2.2	-2.3	+0.1
7.7–12.4	-0.2	-0.4	-0.6	-0.8	-1.0	-1.2	-1.4	-1.6	-1.8	-2.0	-2.2	-2.4	+0.1
12.5–12.7	-0.3	-0.5	-0.7	-0.9	-1.1	-1.3	-1.5	-1.7	-1.9	-2.1	-2.3	-2.5	+0.1
12.8–13.0	-0.3	-0.6	-0.8	-1.0	-1.2	-1.4	-1.6	-1.8	-2.0	-2.2	-2.4	-2.6	+0.1
13.1–13.3	-0.3	-0.6	-0.9	-1.1	-1.3	-1.5	-1.7	-1.9	-2.1	-2.3	-2.5	-2.7	+0.1

13.4–13.6	-0.3	-0.6	-0.9	-1.2	-1.4	-1.6	-1.8	-2.0	-2.2	-2.4	-2.6	-2.8	+0.1
13.7–13.9	-0.3	-0.6	-0.9	-1.2	-1.5	-1.7	-1.9	-2.1	-2.3	-2.5	-2.7	-2.9	+0.1
14.0–14.2	-0.3	-0.6	-0.9	-1.2	-1.5	-1.8	-2.0	-2.2	-2.4	-2.6	-2.8	-3.0	+0.1
14.3–14.5	-0.3	-0.6	-0.9	-1.2	-1.5	-1.8	-2.1	-2.3	-2.5	-2.7	-2.9	-3.1	+0.1
14.6–14.8	-0.3	-0.6	-0.9	-1.2	-1.5	-1.8	-2.1	-2.4	-2.6	-2.8	-3.0	-3.2	+0.1
14.9–15.1	-0.3	-0.6	-0.9	-1.2	-1.5	-1.8	-2.1	-2.4	-2.7	-2.9	-3.1	-3.3	+0.1
15.2–15.4	-0.3	-0.6	-0.9	-1.2	-1.5	-1.8	-2.1	-2.4	-2.7	-3.0	-3.2	-3.4	+0.1
15.5–15.7	-0.3	-0.6	-0.9	-1.2	-1.5	-1.8	-2.1	-2.4	-2.7	-3.0	-3.3	-3.5	+0.1
15.8–20.4	-0.3	-0.6	-0.9	-1.2	-1.5	-1.8	-2.1	-2.4	-2.7	-3.0	-3.3	-3.6	+0.1
20.5–20.8	-0.4	-0.7	-1.0	-1.3	-1.6	-1.9	-2.2	-2.5	-2.8	-3.1	-3.4	-3.7	+0.1
20.9–21.2	-0.4	-0.8	-1.1	-1.4	-1.7	-2.0	-2.3	-2.6	-2.9	-3.2	-3.5	-3.8	+0.1
21.3–21.6	-0.4	-0.8	-1.2	-1.5	-1.8	-2.1	-2.4	-2.7	-3.0	-3.3	-3.6	-3.9	+0.1
21.7–22.0	-0.4	-0.8	-1.2	-1.6	-1.9	-2.2	-2.5	-2.8	-3.1	-3.4	-3.7	-4.0	+0.1
22.1–22.4	-0.4	-0.8	-1.2	-1.6	-2.0	-2.3	-2.6	-2.9	-3.2	-3.5	-3.8	-4.1	+0.1
22.5–22.8	-0.4	-0.8	-1.2	-1.6	-2.0	-2.4	-2.7	-3.0	-3.3	-3.6	-3.9	-4.2	+0.1
22.9–23.2	-0.4	-0.8	-1.2	-1.6	-2.0	-2.4	-2.8	-3.1	-3.4	-3.7	-4.0	-4.3	+0.1
23.3–23.6	-0.4	-0.8	-1.2	-1.6	-2.0	-2.4	-2.8	-3.2	-3.5	-3.8	-4.1	-4.4	+0.1
23.7–24.0	-0.4	-0.8	-1.2	-1.6	-2.0	-2.4	-2.8	-3.2	-3.6	-3.9	-4.2	-4.5	+0.1
24.1–24.4	-0.4	-0.8	-1.2	-1.6	-2.0	-2.4	-2.8	-3.2	-3.6	-4.0	-4.3	-4.6	+0.1
24.5–24.8	-0.4	-0.8	-1.2	-1.6	-2.0	-2.4	-2.8	-3.2	-3.6	-4.0	-4.4	-4.7	+0.1
24.9–28.0	-0.4	-0.8	-1.2	-1.6	-2.0	-2.4	-2.8	-3.2	-3.6	-4.0	-4.4	-4.8	+0.1

Appendix C
Table for converting Par and Stableford scores to nett differentials
(Note – the Table is based on full handicap allowance)

Score versus PAR	7 down	6 down	5 down	4 down	3 down	2 down	1 down	All Square	1 up	2 up	3 up	4 up	5 up	6 up	7 up
STABLEFORD points scored	29	30	31	32	33	34	35	36	37	38	39	40	41	42	43
Par 7 less than CSS −14	0	−1	−2	−3	−4	−5	−6	−7	−8	−9	−10	−11	−12	−13	
Par 6 less than CSS −13	+1	0	−1	−2	−3	−4	−5	−6	−7	−8	−9	−10	−11	−12	
Par 5 less than CSS −12	+2	+1	0	−1	−2	−3	−4	−5	−6	−7	−8	−9	−10	−11	
Par 4 less than CSS −11	+3	+2	+1	0	−1	−2	−3	−4	−5	−6	−7	−8	−9	−10	
Par 3 less than CSS −10	+4	+3	+2	+1	0	−1	−2	−3	−4	−5	−6	−7	−8	−9	
Par 2 less than CSS	+5	+4	+3	+2	+1	0	−1	−2	−3	−4	−5	−6	−7	−8	−9
Par 1 less than CSS	+6	+5	+4	+3	+2	+1	0	−1	−2	−3	−4	−5	−6	−7	−8

	+7	+6	+5	+4	+3	+2	+1	0	-1	-2	-3	-4	-5	-6	-7
Par equal to CSS	+7	+6	+5	+4	+3	+2	+1	0	-1	-2	-3	-4	-5	-6	-7
Par 1 more than CSS	+8	+7	+6	+5	+4	+3	+2	+1	0	-1	-2	-3	-4	-5	-6
Par 2 more than CSS	+9	+8	+7	+6	+5	+4	+3	+2	+1	0	-1	-2	-3	-4	-5
Par 3 more than CSS	+10	+9	+8	+7	+6	+5	+4	+3	+2	+1	0	-1	-2	-3	-4
Par 4 more than CSS	+11	+10	+9	+8	+7	+6	+5	+4	+3	+2	+1	0	-1	-2	-3
Par 5 more than CSS	+12	+11	+10	+9	+8	+7	+6	+5	+4	+3	+2	+1	0	-1	-2
Par 6 more than CSS	+13	+12	+11	+10	+9	+8	+7	+6	+5	+4	+3	+2	+1	0	-1

Example:-
(a) 3 up on a Par 72 course with a CSS of 70. Par is 2 more than CSS so Nett Differential = 1.
(b) 37 Stableford points on a course with Par 68 & CSS 69. Par is 1 less than CSS so Nett Differential = -2.

Appendix D
Standard Scratch Score and
Handicapping Scheme

THE COMPETITION SCRATCH SCORE

Number of Competitors Including No Returns			Percentages		Rounded %
Category 1	A	A x 100/D	F		I
Category 2	B	B x 100/D	G		J
Category 3	C	100 minus boxes I & J			K
Total	D	Total			100
Number of Nett Scores in Categories 1,2 & 3 at 2 over SSS and better	E	E x 100/D	H		L

Procedure

1. Enter in Boxes A, B and C the number of competitors, including no returns, from each of the Categories 1, 2 & 3.

2. Enter the total number of competitors in Categories 1, 2 & 3, **including no returns**, in Box D.

3. Enter in Box E the number of competitors in Categories 1, 2 & 3 who have returned nett scores two over SSS and better. For Par and Stableford competitions use the converted equivalent.

Note: To establish the converted equivalent of a score Two over SSS calculate as follows:

(a) Stableford Competitions = Par less SSS
plus 36 less 2

(b) Par Competitions = Par less SSS
less 2

4. In Boxes F, G and H enter the percentages of the adjacent boxes in relation fo Box D as indicated.

5. Round the number in Box F to the nearest 10% and enter the result in Box I (5% upwards).

6. Round the number in Box G to the nearest 10% and enter the result in Box J (5% upwards).

Note: Occasionally the rounding of Boxes F and G will produce a total of Boxes I and J in excess of 100. When this occurs round the number in Box G downwards and insert the amended number in Box J.

7. Enter in Box K the total of Boxes I and J deducted from 100. (The percentage in Box K may not coincide with the rounded percentage Box C would give if calculated.)

8. Round the number in Box H to the nearest whole number (0.5 upwards) and enter the result in Box L.

9. Select the relevant Table – Table A when the total number of competitors exceeds 30, otherwise Table B. Select the row which contains the percentage shown in Boxes I, J and K.

10 In the row selected find the column which includes the number in Box L. The SSS adjustment is shown in the heading of that column and that number is added to or deducted from the SSS to provide the COMPETITION SCRATCH SCORE ('CSS'). For each QUALIFYING COMPETITION the CSS replaces the SSS for all handicapping purposes. The BUFFER ZONES are applied to the CSS and not the SSS.

11. The heading N/C at the top of a column in the Tables indicates that scores returned shall not result in handicap increases. Reductions of handicap will be made on the basis that the CSS is three strokes higher than the SSS.

12. When a competition has been abandoned for any reason reductions of handicaps shall be on the basis that the CSS is equal to the SSS but no handicaps shall be increased.

13. In the event of all the competitors in a QUALIFYING COMPETITION holding handicaps in CATEGORY 4 the COMPETITION SCRATCH SCORE shall be the STANDARD SCRATCH SCORE.

14. HANDICAP COMMITTEES are reminded that they no longer have a discretion to determine that a QUALIFYING COMPETITION shall or shall not be 'non-counting'.

Appendix E
Table A More than 30 competitors

Categories			Adjustments to SSS to determine the CSS					
1	2	3	N/C	+3	+2	+1	0	-1
0%	0%	100%	0-4	5-7	8-10	11-15	16-30	31+
0%	10%	90%	0-4	5-7	8-11	12-15	16-32	33+
0%	20%	80%	0-5	6-7	8-11	12-16	17-34	35+
0%	30%	70%	0-5	6-8	9-12	13-17	18-36	37+
0%	40%	60%	0-5	6-8	9-12	13-18	19-38	39+
0%	50%	50%	0-5	6-8	9-13	14-19	20-40	41+
0%	60%	40%	0-5	6-9	10-14	15-20	21-41	42+
0%	70%	30%	0-5	6-9	10-14	15-21	22-43	44+
0%	80%	20%	0-5	6-9	10-15	16-22	23-45	46+
0%	90%	10%	0-6	7-10	11-15	16-23	24-47	48+
0%	100%	0%	0-6	7-10	11-16	17-24	25-49	50+
10%	0%	90%	0-5	6-8	9-12	13-17	18-34	35+
10%	10%	80%	0-5	6-8	9-12	13-18	19-36	37+
10%	20%	70%	0-5	6-8	9-13	14-18	19-38	39+
10%	30%	60%	0-5	6-9	10-13	14-19	20-39	40+
10%	40%	50%	0-5	6-9	10-14	15-20	21-41	42+
10%	50%	40%	0-5	6-9	10-14	15-21	22-43	44+
10%	60%	30%	0-6	7-9	10-15	16-22	23-45	46+
10%	70%	20%	0-6	7-10	11-16	17-23	24-27	48+
10%	80%	10%	0-6	7-10	11-16	17-24	25-49	50+
10%	90%	0%	0-6	7-10	11-17	8-25	26-51	52+
20%	0%	80%	0-5	6-8	9-13	14-19	20-38	39+
20%	10%	70%	0-5	6-9	10-14	15-20	21-39	40+
20%	20%	60%	0-5	6-9	10-14	15-21	22-41	42+
20%	30%	50%	0-6	7-9	10-15	16-22	23-43	44+
20%	40%	40%	0-6	7-10	11-15	16-22	23-45	46+
20%	50%	30%	0-6	7-10	11-16	17-23	24-47	48+
20%	60%	20%	0-6	7-10	11-16	17-24	25-49	50+
20%	70%	10%	0-6	7-11	12-17	18-25	26-51	52+
20%	80%	0%	0-6	7-11	12-18	19-26	27-53	54+
30%	0%	70%	0-6	7-9	10-14	15-21	22-41	42+
30%	10%	60%	0-6	7-10	11-15	16-22	23-43	44+
30%	20%	50%	0-6	7-10	11-16	17-23	24-45	46+
I	J	K	VALUES OF L (Percentages)					

Categories			Adjustments to SSS to determine the CSS					
1	2	3	N/C	+3	+2	+1	0	-1
30%	30%	40%	0-6	7-10	11-16	17-24	25-47	48+
30%	40%	30%	0-6	7-11	12-17	18-25	26-49	50+
30%	50%	20%	0-6	7-11	12-17	18-26	27-51	52+
30%	60%	10%	0-6	7-11	12-18	19-26	27-53	54+
30%	70%	0%	0-7	8-11	12-18	19-27	28-55	56+
40%	0%	60%	0-6	7-10	11-16	17-23	24-45	46+
40%	10%	50%	0-6	7-10	11-16	17-24	25-47	48+
40%	20%	40%	0-6	7-11	12-17	18-25	26-49	50+
40%	30%	30%	0-6	7-11	12-18	19-26	27-51	52+
40%	40%	20%	0-7	8-11	12-18	19-27	28-53	54+
40%	50%	10%	0-7	8-12	13-19	20-28	29-55	56+
40%	60%	0%	0-7	8-12	13-19	20-29	30-57	58+
50%	0%	50%	0-6	7-11	12-17	18-25	26-49	50+
50%	10%	40%	0-7	8-11	12-18	19-26	27-51	52+
50%	20%	30%	0-7	8-12	13-18	19-27	28-53	54+
50%	30%	20%	0-7	8-12	13-19	20-28	29-55	56+
50%	40%	10%	0-7	8-12	13-20	21-29	30-57	58+
50%	50%	0%	0-7	8-13	14-20	21-30	31-59	60+
60%	0%	40%	0-7	8-12	13-19	20-27	28-53	54+
60%	10%	30%	0-7	8-12	13-19	20-28	29-55	56+
60%	20%	20%	0-7	8-12	13-20	21-29	30-57	58+
60%	30%	10%	0-7	8-13	14-20	21-30	31-59	60+
60%	40%	0%	0-7	8-13	14-21	22-31	32-61	62+
70%	0%	30%	0-7	8-13	14-20	21-30	31-57	58+
70%	10%	20%	0-7	8-13	14-21	22-31	32-59	60+
70%	20%	10%	0-8	9-13	14-21	22-31	32-60	61+
70%	30%	0%	0-8	9-14	15-22	23-32	33-62	63+
80%	0%	20%	0-8	9-13	14-22	23-32	33-60	61+
80%	10%	10%	0-8	9-14	15-22	23-33	34-62	63+
80%	20%	0%	0-8	9-14	15-23	24-34	35-64	65+
90%	0%	10%	0-8	9-14	15-23	24-34	35-64	65+
90%	10%	0%	0-8	9-15	16-24	25-35	36-66	67+
100%	0%	0%	0-9	10-15	16-24	25-36	37-68	69+
I	J	K	VALUES OF L (Percentages)					

Appendix F
Table A More than 31 competitors

Categories			Adjustments to SSS to determine the CSS					
1	2	3	N/C	+3	+2	+1	0	-1
0%	0%	100%	0-3	4-5	6-8	9-12	13-30	31+
0%	10%	90%	0-3	4-6	7-9	10-13	14-32	33+
0%	20%	80%	0-3	4-6	7-9	10-14	15-34	35+
0%	30%	70%	0-4	5-6	7-10	11-14	15-36	37+
0%	40%	60%	0-4	5-6	7-10	11-15	16-38	39+
0%	50%	50%	0-4	5-7	8-10	11-16	17-40	41+
0%	60%	40%	0-4	5-7	8-11	12-17	18-41	42+
0%	70%	30%	0-4	5-7	8-11	12-17	18-43	44+
0%	80%	20%	0-4	5-7	8-12	13-18	19-45	46+
0%	90%	10%	0-4	5-7	8-12	13-19	20-47	48+
0%	100%	0%	0-4	5-8	9-13	14-19	20-49	50+
10%	0%	90%	0-4	5-6	7-9	10-14	15-34	35+
10%	10%	80%	0-4	5-6	7-10	11-15	16-36	37+
10%	20%	70%	0-4	5-6	7-10	11-15	16-38	39+
10%	30%	60%	0-4	5-7	8-11	12-16	17-39	40+
10%	40%	50%	0-4	5-7	8-11	12-17	18-41	42+
10%	50%	40%	0-4	5-7	8-12	13-18	19-43	44+
10%	60%	30%	0-4	5-7	8-12	13-18	19-45	46+
10%	70%	20%	0-4	5-8	9-12	13-19	20-47	48+
10%	80%	10%	0-4	5-8	9-13	14-20	21-49	50+
10%	90%	0%	0-4	5-8	9-13	14-20	21-51	52+
20%	0%	80%	0-4	5-7	8-11	12-16	17-38	39+
20%	10%	70%	0-4	5-7	8-11	12-16	17-39	40+
20%	20%	60%	0-4	5-7	8-11	12-17	18-41	42+
20%	30%	50%	0-4	5-7	8-12	13-18	19-43	44+
20%	40%	40%	0-4	5-7	8-12	13-19	20-45	46+
20%	50%	30%	0-4	5-8	9-13	14-19	20-47	48+
20%	60%	20%	0-4	5-8	9-13	14-20	21-49	50+
20%	70%	10%	0-4	5-8	9-13	14-21	22-51	52+
20%	80%	0%	0-5	6-8	9-14	15-22	23-53	54+
30%	0%	70%	0-4	5-7	8-12	13-18	19-41	42+
30%	10%	60%	0-4	5-7	8-12	13-18	19-43	44+
30%	20%	50%	0-4	5-8	9-12	13-19	20-45	46+
I	J	K	VALUES OF L (Percentages)					

Categories			Adjustments to SSS to determine the CSS					
1	2	3	N/C	+3	+2	+1	0	-1
30%	30%	40%	0-4	5-8	9-13	14-20	21-47	48+
30%	40%	30%	0-4	5-8	9-13	14-20	21-49	50+
30%	50%	20%	0-5	6-8	9-14	15-21	22-51	52+
30%	60%	10%	0-5	6-9	10-14	15-22	23-53	54+
30%	70%	0%	0-5	6-9	10-15	16-23	24-55	56+
40%	0%	60%	0-4	5-8	9-13	14-19	20-45	46+
40%	10%	50%	0-4	5-8	9-13	14-20	21-47	48+
40%	20%	40%	0-5	6-8	9-14	15-21	22-49	50+
40%	30%	30%	0-5	6-8	9-14	15-21	22-51	52+
40%	40%	20%	0-5	6-9	10-14	15-22	23-53	54+
40%	50%	10%	0-5	6-9	10-15	16-23	24-55	56+
40%	60%	0%	0-5	6-9	10-15	16-24	24-57	58+
50%	0%	50%	0-5	6-8	9-14	15-21	22-49	50+
50%	10%	40%	0-5	6-9	10-14	15-22	23-51	52+
50%	20%	30%	0-5	6-9	10-15	16-22	23-53	54+
50%	30%	20%	0-5	6-9	10-15	16-23	24-55	56+
50%	40%	10%	0-5	6-9	10-16	17-24	25-57	58+
50%	50%	0%	0-5	6-10	11-16	17-25	26-59	60+
60%	0%	40%	0-5	6-9	10-15	16-23	24-53	54+
60%	10%	30%	0-5	6-9	10-15	16-24	25-55	56+
60%	20%	20%	0-5	6-9	10-16	17-24	25-57	58+
60%	30%	10%	0-5	6-10	11-16	17-25	26-59	60+
60%	40%	0%	0-5	6-10	11-17	18-26	27-61	62+
70%	0%	30%	0-5	6-10	11-16	17-25	26-57	58+
70%	10%	20%	0-5	6-10	11-16	17-25	26-59	60+
70%	20%	10%	0-5	6-10	11-17	18-26	27-60	61+
70%	30%	0%	0-5	6-10	11-17	18-27	28-62	63+
80%	0%	20%	0-5	6-10	11-17	18-26	27-60	61+
80%	10%	10%	0-6	7-10	11-18	19-27	28-62	63+
80%	20%	0%	0-6	7-11	12-18	19-28	29-64	65+
90%	0%	10%	0-6	7-11	12-18	19-28	29-64	65+
90%	10%	0%	0-6	7-11	12-19	20-29	30-66	67+
100%	0%	0%	0-6	7-11	12-19	20-30	31-68	69+
I	J	K	VALUES OF L (Percentages)					

Appendix G
Handicap Allowances
As recommended by Council of National Golf Unions

The Council of National Golf Unions recommends that the following handicap allowances shall apply in the following forms of play. The reference to handicaps in all cases refers to PLAYING HANDICAPS.

Match-Play

Singles The full difference between the HANDICAPS of the two players

Foursomes $\frac{1}{2}$ of the full difference between the aggregate HANDICAP of either side

Four-ball (better ball) Back marker to concede strokes to the other three players based on $\frac{3}{4}$ of the difference between the full handicap.

Strokes to be taken according to the Stroke Table.

Bogey or Par Competitions

Singles Full handicap

Foursomes $\frac{1}{2}$ of the aggregate HANDICAP of the partners.

Four-ball (better ball) Each partner receives $\frac{3}{4}$ of full handicap.

Strokes to be taken according to the Stroke Table.

Stroke-Play

Singles Full handicap

Foursomes $\frac{1}{2}$ of aggregate HANDICAPS of the partners.

Four-ball (better ball) Each partner receives $\frac{3}{4}$ of the full handicap and strokes to be taken according to the Stroke Table.

Stableford Competitions

Singles Full handicap

Foursomes $\frac{1}{2}$ of aggregate HANDICAPS of the partners.

Four-ball (better ball) Each partner receives $\frac{3}{4}$ of full handicap.

Strokes to be taken according to the Stroke Table and not added to the points scored.

Note 1: Half Strokes. Half strokes or over to be counted as one; smaller fractions to be disregarded.

Note 2: Handicap allowances in a handicap competition must be laid down by the Committee in the Conditions of the Competition (Rules of Golf 33-1).

Note 3: 36 hole competitions. In handicap competitions over 36 holes, strokes should be given or taken in accordance with the 18 hole Stroke Table unless the Committee introduces a special Stroke Table.

Note 4: Sudden death play-off. When extra holes are played in handicap competitions, strokes should be taken in accordance with the Stroke Table.

Appendix H
Computer Software Relating to
The Standard Scratch and Handicapping
Scheme

With effect from 1 January 1994 any software used by Affiliated Clubs shall provide a printed record for submission, when required, to Area Authorities or National Unions which contain all of the following information

1. The name of the Affiliated Club.
2. The name of the Player.
3. The Player's Home Club.
4. The name of any other Clubs of which the Player is a member.
5. The Player's Exact Handicap held immediately before the entry for the first Qualifying Competition shown in the records.
6. The date of each Qualifying Competition.
7. The Nett Differential in each Qualifying Competition or an entry identifying a 'No Return'.
8. All entries must be displayed and handicap adjustments made in chronological order.
9. The Exact Handicap and the Playing Handicap must be shown after each Qualifying Competition.
10. An identification of Nett Differentials returned elsewhere than the Player's Home Club.

11. Identification of any handicap adjustments made pursuant to Clause 19.

12. A statement of the frequency of upward revisions of Playing Handicaps (Clause 16(10)).

Appendix I
Decisions

1. Scores in Extended Competitions

If from a series of any number of scores special prizes are awarded for the best eclectic score or the best nett or gross aggregate of a prescribed number of scores, the individual scores in the series will be QUALIFYING COMPETITIONS provided each score is returned under MEDAL PLAY CONDITIONS in a QUALIFYING COMPETITION, as defined in the Scheme, and not returned solely for the purpose of the eclectic, nett or gross aggregate awards.

2. Qualifying Scores

(a) If a club with a large number of QUALIFYING COMPETITIONS in the calendar year wishes to deprive certain of the competitions of their status as QUALIFYING COMPETITIONS it may do so provided competitors are so advised before play commences.

(b) It would be outside the spirit of the Handicapping Scheme to declare that all Club Medal Competitions during a specified period would not be regarded as QUALIFYING COMPETITIONS, although played under full MEDAL PLAY CONDITIONS.

(c) In both (a) and (b) above it would be more appropriate to play unofficial MEDAL COMPETITIONS under conditions which would not give them the status of QUALIFYING COMPETITIONS.

Note: A declaration that a competition is not a QUALIFYING COMPETITION disqualifies all scores returned in that competition for handicapping purposes, Thus a player returning a score below his handicap will not have his EXACT HANDICAP reduced nor will a score above a player's

BUFFER ZONE increase his EXACT HANDICAP. Clause 19(4)(b) does however allow scores in non-qualifying competitions to be one of a number of considerations when deciding to effect or recommend a handicap adjustment.

(d) A competition will not lose the status of QUALIFY-ING COMPETITION when played under conditions when, because of work proceeding or ground condi-tions in the area, pegging-up has been made obliga-tory by the club on a restricted area of the course, provided the playing of QUALIFYING COMPETI-TIONS under such conditions has the prior approval of the UNION or AREA AUTHORITY.

3. Upwards adjustment of Handicaps

(a) Clubs may elect to adjust PLAYING HANDICAPS upwards at the end of each calendar month or at shorter intervals, including immediate adjustment after completion of each QUALIFYING COMPETI-TION at the club.

(b) There could be slight differences in EXACT HANDI-CAPS produced by each method when comparison is made at the end of a calendar month.

(c) The procedure for recording NETT DIFFERENTIALS set out in the Scheme should be adhered to whatev-er method is used.

(d) There is no objection to clubs electing to adjust PLAYING HANDICAPS upwards at the end of each calendar month, or at more frequent intervals, tak-ing steps to adjust and record EXACT and PLAYING HANDICAPS so that at the end of each month they correspond with those derived by adjusting handi-caps after the playing of each QUALIFYING COM-PETITON.

4. Limitation of Handicaps

Clubs have inquired whether they may impose a limit of handicap to some of their competitions eg insist that a 24 handicap player competes from a handicap of 18. This is permitted by Rule of Golf 33-1. However, when recording the players' scores for handicapping purposes, adjustments must be made to ensure that the NETT DIFFERENTIAL is recorded from his current PLAYING HANDICAP ie in the example quoted 24 instead of 18.

This is comparatively simple for MEDAL COMPETITION, but is impractical for Stableford and Par competitions as it is unlikely for example that a player would record a score at a hole where a stroke allowance of one from an 18 handicap gave him no points, whereas from a handicap of 24 with a stroke allowance of two at that particular hole he might have registered one point.

5. Incomplete Cards and No Returns

(a) All cards must be returned, whether complete or not.

(b) It is expected that every player who enters for an 18 hole QUALIFYING COMPETITION intends to complete the round.

(c) Since an Incomplete Card and a No Return have the effect of increasing a player's handicap, the club would be justified in refusing to accept a card or record a 'N.R.' when the player has walked in after playing only a few holes.

(d) Cards should not be issued to players when there is obviously insufficient light for them to complete the round.

(e) Sympathetic consideration should be given to players who have had to discontinue play for any cause considered to be reasonable by the organising committee.

(f) Clauses 17 and 19 of the Scheme give clubs the discretion to deal with players who persistently submit Incomplete Cards or make No Returns if they consider they are attempting to 'build a handicap'.

6. Reduction of Handicaps during a Competition

Where the conditions of a competition do not provide otherwise the handicap of a player applying at the beginning of a competition shall apply throughout that competition. This provision shall apply to a competition in which supplementary prizes are awarded for the best scores returned in an individual round or in combinations of individual rounds of the competition. The provisions shall not apply in circumstances where the winner is the player returning the lowest aggregate score in two or more separate competitions.

Where a player's handicap has been reduced during the course of a competition in which the original handicap continues to apply the player shall play from his reduced handicap in all other competitions commencing after the handicap reduction.

7. Overseas Scores

Scores returned in tournaments organised by the European Golf Association are QUALIFYING SCORES for handicapping purposes and must be returned to the HOME CLUB pursuant to clause 13.(7) provided COMPETITION SCRATCH SCORES have been calculated. Other scores returned in overseas tournaments may be returned and used, if considered appropriate, under the terms of clause 19.

8. Clause 19

Reductions pursuant to Clause 19 can be made only when the HANDICAP COMMITTEE has reason to believe that the handicap of a player may be too high. The Committee must consider all available information regarding the player's ability. A low score in a single event is not sufficient evidence alone to justify a Clause 19 reduction.

If the handicap of any player is reduced other than to the extent required by Clause 16 or by the correct application of Clause 19, the player's handicap will not be a CONGU handicap and cannot be used in any competition for which a CONGU handicap is required.

Stationery

Enquiries regarding storage binders and handicap record sheets suitable for use in connection with the Standard Scratch Score and Handicapping Scheme 1983 to be directed to Hon Secretary of the Council of National Golf Unions: A. Thirlwell, 19 Birch Green, Formby, Liverpool L37 1NG.

Forms of application for:
An alteration to the Basic Standard Scratch Score.

An addition for course value to the Provisional Standard Scratch Score.

The above forms may be obtained from the Secretaries of:

(a) County Golf Unions or District Committees.

(b) Area Authorities.

(c) National Golf Unions.

(d) Council of National Golf Unions.

DRAWS FOR MATCH PLAY COMPETITIONS

Cold Draw

When the number of entries is not a whole power of 2, i.e. 4, 8, 16, 32, 64 etc, a number of first round byes are necessary. Subtract the number of entries from the nearest of these numbers above the number of entries to give the number of byes. *Example:* (a) 28 entries – subtracting from 32 gives 4 first round byes; (b) 33 entries – subtracting from 64 gives 31 first round byes.

All names (or numbers representing names) are put in a hat and the requisite number of byes drawn out singly and placed in pairs in the second round of the draw, alternately at the top and bottom, ie the first two names go at the top of the draw, the next two at the bottom and so on until all the byes have been drawn. If there is an odd number of byes, the last drawn is bracketed to play against the winner of either the first or last first round match. Having drawn all the byes, the remaining names are then drawn and placed in pairs in the first round in the order drawn in the middle of the draw.

Automatic Draw

When a stroke-play qualifying round(s) is used to determine the qualifiers for the ensuing match-play, the automatic draw is used, based on the qualifying position of each qualifier, ie the leading qualifier is number 1 in the draw, the second qualifier is number 2 and so on.

The following table gives the automatic draw for up to 64 qualifiers. Use the first column for 64 qualifiers, the second column for 32 qualifiers, and so on.

1/64	1	1	1	1	1
33/32	32				
17/48	17	16			
49/16	16				
9/56	9	9	8		
41/24	24				
25/40	25	8			
57/8	8				
5/60	5	5	5	4	
37/28	28				
21/44	21	12			
53/12	12				
13/52	13	13	4		
45/20	20				
29/36	29	4			
61/4	4				
3/62	3	3	3	3	2
35/30	30				
19/46	19	14			
51/14	14				
11/54	11	11	6		
43/22	22				
27/38	27	6			
59/6	6				
7/58	7	7	7	2	
39/26	26				
23/42	23	10			
55/10	10				
15/50	15	15	2		
47/18	18				
31/34	31	2			
63/2	2				

THE LADIES' GOLF UNION SCRATCH SCORE AND HANDICAPPING SCHEME

Effective from 1 February 1994

CONTENTS

SECTION I
DEFINITIONS

Average differential
The sum of the differentials divided by their number.

Bona fide Society
A society which meets the following LGU criteria, and is thereby permitted to organise Qualifying Competitions for its members:

(a) The society must have a committee with annually elected officers including a Secretary conversant with LGU handicapping regulations.

(b) Members must have an authentic golfing bond such as in Girls', Past Lady Captains' and Seniors' Golfing Societies, or a common bond through the members' professions or businesses, such as the National Westminster Bank Golfing Society for Bank employees.

Completed Gross Score
The term used to distinguish a total 18 hole gross score when a gross score has been recorded for each hole, from a Converted Gross Score. The card must be checked, signed by the marker and countersigned by the player. The card should also show the player's name and the date.

Converted Gross Score
The total 18 hole gross score converted from the points scored in Stableford Qualifying Competition, or the result against par in Par Qualifying Competition. The card must be checked, signed by the marker and countersigned by the player. The card should also show the player's name and the date.

Committee
The term 'Committee' is deemed to refer to the Committee of the Ladies' Section. The term 'Club Committee' refers to the Committee in charge of the course. Where the management of the club and/or course is entirely in the hands of the Ladies' Committee the term 'Club Committee' shall be deemed to refer to such.

Differential
The difference between the total gross score and the Scratch Score of the course on which it is returned.

Extra Day Score
A Completed Gross Score which is returned other than in Qualifying Competition. The card should be marked 'EDS' (even when returning in a non-qualifying event).

Handicap Advisers
Handicap Advisers and their Deputies are persons appointed by the National Organisation to assist Handicap Secretaries in dealing with problems and exceptional cases, and to keep records of all players with handicaps under 4.

Handicap Secretary
A player's Handicap Secretary is the Handicap Secretary of her Home Club. The Handicap Secretary of an Individual Member of the LGU, or of a National Organisation, is the Administrator of the LGU or the Secretary of the National Organisation respectively. The Handicap Secretary of a visitor from overseas, unless she joins an affiliated club as an annual member, is the Administrator of the LGU.

Home Club
The Home Club is the club which a member of more than one club has chosen to be that where her handicap records shall be maintained and of which the Handicap Secretary shall be her Handicap Secretary.

Home/Away Courses
Home Course Any course situated at, and associated with, a club at which the player has club membership. (Except at her Home Club a course at which a player holds Honorary club membership shall count as an Away Course in a Qualifying Competition open to non-members.)
Away Course A course at which a player has no club membership.

Individual Members
  (a) *of the* LGU: Players temporarily resident overseas, for

a period of not less than one year, are entitled to apply for individual membership of the LGU.

(b) *of the National Organisations:* Players unable to become an annual playing member of an affiliated club may apply to their National Organisation for individual membership.

Lapsed Handicap

A handicap has lapsed if four scores have not been returned in an LGU year by Category C, D and E players, six scores in Qualifying Competitions by Category B players (unless increasing to Category C) and ten scores in Qualifying Competitions by Category A players (unless increasing to Category B).

LGU Medal Competition

LGU Medal Competitions are designated Stroke-Play Competitions. Any number to a maximum of sixteen may be held and may be played in conjunction with club stroke-play competitions authorised by the Committee. A minimum of four cards must be returned to qualify for the annual Silver and Bronze Medals.

LGU Tees and Teeing Grounds

The LGU tees, indicated by a Permanent Marker on the right hand side of the tee, are those from which the Scratch Score has been fixed. The actual teeing ground in play (see Rules of Golf Definition) is indicated by red tee markers which, for the convenience of the greenkeeper, may be moved in any direction from the Permanent Marker provided the hole is not altered in length by more than ten yards.

Note: In the event of the teeing ground having been accidentally or otherwise moved beyond the permitted limit the score cannot count for handicap or for LGU Competitions unless a special Scratch Score is allotted by the National Organisation.

Live Score

A score returned (in accordance with Regulation III.4) in the current LGU year (1 February to 31 January) or in the preceding LGU year.

National Organisation

The National Organisations are: the English Ladies' Golf Association, the Irish Ladies' Golf Union, the Scottish Ladies' Golfing Association and the Welsh Ladies' Golf Union. In the case of overseas affiliated clubs, for 'National Organisation' read 'LGU'.

Qualifying Competition

A stroke competition held on a specified day arranged with Club Committee permission.

Qualifying Competition Score

A gross score returned in a Qualifying Competition which counts as a competition score for LGU handicap purposes.

Scratch Score

The Scratch Score of a course is the score expected of a Scratch player in normal Spring and Autumn conditions of wind and weather.

Symbols

@ – marks a regained handicap in Categories A and B only, which has had to be assessed rather than calculated because the required types of score have not been returned.

* – asterisk – marks a handicap when the result of the calculation has been limited by the regulations. P – marks a handicap when the player is not eligible to play in LGU Medal Competitions.

SECTION II
INTRODUCTION

1. Basis of the System

The chief features of the LGU System of Handicapping are: that all handicaps shall be fixed on the basis of the LGU Scratch Score; that handicaps shall be assessed on actual scores returned and not on general form; and that the player's LGU handicap shall be the same in every club.

2. Overseas Unions and Clubs

Overseas affiliated Unions and Clubs shall be permitted to

make such adjustments to these regulations as may be deemed by their Executive Committee to be necessary on account of climatic or other conditions peculiar to the territory adminstered by them, so long as these adjustments do not depart from the fundamental principles of the LGU System of Handicapping as stated in the paragraph above or contravene the Rules of Golf as laid down by the Royal & Ancient Golf Club of St Andrews. The LGU must be informed as and when such adjustments are made.

3. Queries

Queries on LGU Regulations shall be, and on the Rules of Golf may be, submitted in accordance with the following procedures:

(a) **SECRETARIES and COMMITTEES of Affiliated Clubs** should submit queries to their Handicap Adviser and National Organisation in that order. Handicap queries should be referred to the Club Handicap Secretary, the Handicap Adviser and the National Organisation in that order.

(b) **MEMBERS OF AFFILIATED CLUBS** may submit queries to their National Organisation and must have their statements signed as read on behalf of the Ladies' Committee. If there is any difference of opinion the Committee or opposing party should submit their own statement in writing.

(c) **OVERSEAS UNIONS and CLUBS.** In the case of clubs affiliated to the Ladies' Golf Union outside Great Britain and Ireland or directly affiliated to the LGU, queries should be submitted to the LGU. Statements should be signed as read on behalf of such Union or Club Committee.

Correspondence of this nature sent to the LGU and the National Organisations is filed for reference and cannot be returned.

SECTION III

THE PLAYER'S RESPONSIBILITIES AND RIGHTS

1. General

Playing off the Correct Handicap. It is the player's responsibility to know and to apply the Handicapping Regulations and to play off the correct handicap at all times. The card of any score which might affect the handicap must be returned to the player's Handicap Secretary as soon as possible. She should be able to produce a current Handicap Certificate when required to do so. In case of doubt or disagreement between the player and her Handicap Secretary as to what is the player's correct handicap, she should play off the lower until an official decision can be obtained from the Handicap Adviser or the National Organisation.

Handicap Reduction. Any reduction in handicap is automatic and comes into force immediately, except:

(i) In the event of a tie in a competition which has been completed in one day or on consecutive days, where this is resolved by a replay or a play-off; and

(ii) in a 36, 54 or 72 hole competition played on the same day or on consecutive days.

Playing away from Home. A player must notify her Handicap Secretary of any score (which might affect her handicap) returned by her on any course other than at her Home Club.

2. Eligibility to Hold an LGU Handicap

An LGU handicap may be obtained and held by an amateur lady golfer who is either:

(a) an annual playing member, including a five day, country, junior or life member (whether honorary or paying) of a club affiliated to the LGU either directly or through its National Organisation; or

(b) an Individual Member of either the LGU or one of the four National Organisations; or

(c) a temporary member of an affiliated club, provided her membership is to last for a period of not less than twelve months.

Note: Should membership cease or expire the player's LGU handicap is no longer valid, but her scores remain **LIVE** if returned before such cessation or expiry.

3. How to Gain an LGU Handicap

Four Extra Day Scores must be returned on the course or courses of an LGU affiliated club or clubs, the Scratch Score of which must be not less than 60. Play must be in twos (threes and fours are not acceptable), no more than one player per marker, and must be in accordance with Regulations III4.(a), (b), (c), (d) and (e).

Overseas players joining an LGU affiliated club who hold or have held a recognised handicap. Four live scores returned on an LGU affiliated course must be submitted to the LGU Administrator with the current overseas handicap certificate or information of the handicap last held and the year of lapse. Live scores from non-LGU-affiliated courses overseas which might affect the handicap should be enclosed with course particulars as detailed in the Note to Regulation III4.(b) below. In any event the LGU handicap shall be no higher than a current CONGU or USGA handicap, or the equivalent figure in the case of a lapsed handicap after application of Table II, the Table of Permitted Increases for Lapsed Handicaps.

4. Scores Acceptable for LGU Handicap

To be acceptable for handicap:

(a) Scores must be returned in accordance with the Rules of Golf as approved by the Royal & Ancient Golf Club of St Andrews and with the Club's Local Rules and Bye-Laws, which must not contravene any R&A, Rule or LGU Regulation.

Only scores returned in Qualifying Competitions are acceptable as competition scores for LGU Handicap purposes.

(b) Scores must be returned on the course of an LGU affiliated club with an LGU Scratch Score of not less than 60. Play must be from **LGU TEES**. Extra Day Scores returned on a course of which the player is not a member must be countersigned by a local official to certify that the Scratch Score is correctly stated. Completed cards should either be returned in person by the player to her Handicap Secretary without delay or left in the card box of the club visited, with the name and address of the home club and the cost of postage. Qualifying Competition Scores returned on a course of which a player has no membership must be signed by an official of the Competition Committee who must have confirmed the Scratch Score of the day with the Secretary of the host club.

Note: Scores returned on non-LGU-affiliated courses overseas (see lists in the Lady Golfers' Handbook) may count for handicap at the discretion of the LGU. Such cards, duly countersigned by a local official as showing the correct Scratch Score and accompanied by relevant information about local conditions, type of soil, terrain, course difficulties, etc should be forwarded to the Administrator, LGU, The Scores, St Andrews, Fife, KY16 9AT, with a stamped addressed envelope to the Handicap Secretary of the player's Home Club.

(c) Scores must be marked by an annual playing member of a recognised golf club or an Individual Member (see Definitions) who has or has had a handicap. A marker should not mark the card of more than one player.

(d) A score must be that of the first round of the day on any one course, except in the case of a Qualifying Competition consisting of 36 holes played on one day, when both scores shall count.

(e) **ADVERSE CONDITIONS** – (See Rules of Golf Appendix 1-4) **Local Rules for the Preservation of the Course**

Scores may be returned when the following conditions apply:

(i) Where the Club Committee has made a local rule that the ball may be placed without penalty through the green.

(ii) Where the Club Committee has made a local rule that tee pegs must be used on any closely mown area or through the green:

    (1) A deduction from the Scratch Score of two strokes must be made where more than nine holes are affected.

    (2) A deduction from the Scratch Score of one stroke must be made where nine holes are affected.

    (3) A deduction from the Scratch Score of one stroke will be at the discretion of the area Scratch Score Assessor where fewer than three holes are affected.

In the case of (ii) (1), (2) and (3) the area Scratch Score Assessor **MUST** be notified.

(iii) **The Green**. Where, for the preservation of the green, a temporary hole (see Rules of Golf Definitions) is off but adjacent to the green, provided this does not alter the length of the hole by more than ten yards.

Note: **LGU TEES.** Where, for the preservation of the course, the teeing ground has been moved beyond the permitted ten yards, scores may count for handicap only if a special Scratch Score is allotted by the National Organisation.

(f) Completed Gross Scores, returned in a stroke competition from which a player has been disqualified under R&A Rule 6–2b on her nett score, shall count for handicap.

In Stableford and Par Qualifying Competitions, if no handicap is recorded on the card before it is returned, or if the recorded handicap is higher than that to which a competitor is entitled and this affects the number of strokes received, the player shall be disqualified under R&A Rule 6–2b. The results shall be adjusted according to the player's correct handicap and, on being converted, the Converted Gross Score shall count for handicap.

(g) **SOCIETY DAY COMPETITIONS.** Handicap Secretaries must accept a score returned from a Society Day competition as a Qualifying Competition Score if they are satisfied the society is *bona fide* (see LGU definition of a Bona fide Society).

(h) All scores returned in Stroke Competitions, even if the competition is declared null and void, count for LGU handicap purposes, subject to Regulations III4(a) to (g) above and provided competitors play from **LGU Tees** (see Definition and Note) and the SS of the course is not less than 60. Scores may be returned in twos, threes or fours, as arranged by the Committee.

Note: The exception to this is in a competition where the best-ball or better-ball score (see Rules of Golf Definitions) is to count, and in Pro-Am and Am-Am team events.

(i) **EXTRA DAY SCORES** must be returned in accordance with Regulations III4.(a) to (e) and should normally be marked in twos, but at the discretion of the Committee may be marked in threes or fours, in which case a notice to this effect must be posted on the Notice Board (but see Regulation III3. for gaining a first handicap). The player's name and the date must be recorded on the scorecard.

5. Calculation of LGU Handicap
(a) General

Handicaps are divided into five categories: Silver Division –

A, B, C and Bronze Division – D and E. Handicaps are calculated as follows, on the basis of live scores returned in accordance with Regulation III4. above:

Note 1: For all handicaps, scores must be returned on courses with a Scratch Score of not less than 60.

Note 2: In all calculations above Scratch $^1/_2$, $^2/_3$ and $^3/_4$ count as 1 and $^1/_3$, $^1/_4$ count as 0. In all calculations below scratch, fractions of $^1/_2$ and less count as 0, fractions greater than $^1/_2$ count as 1.

(i) Bronze Division

Category E, 36*–30. The handicap is the difference between the player's best live score and the Scratch Score of the course on which it was played, ie the handicap is her best **DIFFERENTIAL**. If the differential is more than 36 the handicap is 36★ *(Example E¹)* or 36★P (see Regulation IV2.(a)). If the differential is 36-30 then that is the handicap *(Example E²)*. If the best differential is less than 30, the handicap is 30 until the average of the two best differentials is less than 29$^1/_2$ *(Example E³)*.

EXAMPLES

E^1	Best gross score	115 SS 72	Differential	43	
					Handicap 36★
E^2	Best gross score	102 SS 69	Differential	33	
					Handicap 33
E^3	Best gross score	101 SS 74	Differential	27	
		106 SS 70	Previous best differential	36	

AVERAGE DIFFERENTIAL   31$^1/_2$
Handicap 30

Category D, 29–19. The handicap is the average of the two best differentials *(Examples D¹, D²)*, but if the average is less than 18$^1/_2$ the handicap is 19 until the average of the **four** best differentials is less than 18$^1/_2$ *(Example D³)*.

EXAMPLES

D^1	Gross score	99 SS 73	Best differential	26
	Gross score	104 SS 73	Previous best differential	31

Average differential   28$^1/_2$
Handicap 29

D^2	Gross score	95 SS 71	Best differential 24
	Gross score	98 SS 70	Previous best
			differential 28
		Average differential	26
			Handicap 26

D^3	Gross score		Best differentials
		87 SS 72	15
		92 SS 72	20
		Average differential	$17^1/_2$
		but . . . Handicap 19	

		96 SS 73	23
		94 SS 71	23
		Average differential (of four) $20^1/_4$	
		Handicap 19	

(ii) Silver Division

Category C, 18–10. The handicap is the average of the four best differentials *(Example C¹)*, but if this average is less than $9^1/_2$, the handicap is 10 until the conditions for Category B are fulfilled *(Example C²)*.

EXAMPLES
C^1 Best differentials:
   10
   11
   13
   17   Average $12^3/_4$ Handicap 13

C^2 EDS = Extra Day Scores;
   QCS = Qualifying Competition Scores.
   Best differentials:
        10 (EDS)
         9 (QCS)
         7 (EDS)
         6 (QCS)   Average 8 but . . . Handicap 10

        11 (QCS)
        13 (QCS)
        12 (QCS)
        14 (QCS)
     Average differential of six Qualifying Competition
              Scores = $10^5/_6$
                        Handicap 10

Category B, 9–4. The handicap is the average of the six best differentials of scores returned in Qualifying Competitions

(Example B¹), but if this average is less than 3¹/₂, the handicap is 4 until the conditions for Category A are fulfilled *(Example B²)*

EXAMPLES
D^1 Best differentials from Qualifying Competition Scores:

7	
5	
5	
6	
4	
4	Average differential 5¹/₆ Handicap 5

D^2 Best differentials from Qualifying Competition Scores:
H1.H2 = HOME COURSES, A1, A2 etc = Away Courses:

3(H1)	
5(H2)	
4(H1)	
2(H1)	
2(H1)	
3(A1)	Average differential 3¹/₆ but . . . Handicap 4
6(A1)	
7(A2)	
6(H2)	
8(A1)	Average differential 4.6 Handicap 4

Category A, 3 and under. To obtain a handicap of 3 or under, a player must return at least ten scores in Qualifying Competitions. Only six of these scores may be from a Home Course, and the remaining four must be from at least two different Away Courses. The handicap is the average of the ten best differentials so obtained *(Examples A¹ and A²)*.

EXAMPLE: *(Abbreviations as in B²)*

A^1 Best differentials from Qualifying Competition Scores:

0 (H)	
−1 (H	
−1 (H)	
0 (H)	
3 (H)	
0 (H)	
1 (A1)	
0 (A1)	
1 (A2)	
3 (A2)	Average differential 0.6 Handicap 1

A^2 Best differentials from Qualifying Competition Scores:

−1 (H)
−1 (H)
−2 (H)
 1 (A1)
−2 (H)
−1 (A2)
 0 (H)
−1 (H)
 2 (A3)
 0 (A1)   Average differential −0.5

Handicap Scratch (−0.5 = 0)

(b) Stableford and Par Qualifying Competitions

(It is recommended that at least 50% of stroke competitions should be Stroke-Play competitions, ie those where a Completed Gross Score must be returned.)

Where no point is recorded for any hole in a Stableford Qualifying Competition, or a loss is recorded for any hole in a Par Qualifying Competition, the Conversion Chart/formulae MUST be used in arriving at a Converted Gross Score.

Note: Conversion Charts specific to the total PAR of a course (not the SSS) are obtainable from the National Organisation.

Conversion of Stableford Qualifying Scores to Converted Gross Scores

Formula:	Stableford		Full		Converted
Par + 36 −	points scored	+	Handicap	=	Gross Score
Example:					
73 + 36 −	38	+	20	=	91

Conversion of Par Qualifying Scores to Converted Gross Scores

(1) Holes Up

Formula:	Holes		Full		Converted
Par −	up	+	Handicap	=	Gross Score
Example:					
73 −	1	+	20	=	92

(2) All Square

Formula:

Par + Full Handicap = Converted Gross Score

Example:

73 + 20 = 93

(3) Holes Down

Formula:

Par + Holes down + Full Handicap = Converted Gross Score

Example:

73 + 1 + 20 = 94

The above formulae may be applied ONLY to 18 hole Qualifying Competitions and multiples thereof.

Stableford and Par Qualifying Competitions must be played off full handicap.

Stableford and Par Qualifying Competitions must not be combined with Stroke-Play Qualifying Competitions.

Where an overall handicap limit is in force, such handicap, if lower than the player's handicap, is that which must be recorded on the card. In Stableford and Par Qualifying Competitions, such handicap must be used when converting to the Converted Gross Score.

6. Annual Revision of Handicaps and LAPSED HANDICAPS

(a) General

On 31 January each year all handicaps shall be recalculated on the basis of scores returned during the preceding twelve months and in accordance with the Regulations in force during that period. Any increase in handicap resulting from such recalculation shall be limited by Table I – Table of Permitted Increases for Revised Handicaps set out below. At no other time during the year may a player's handicap be increased (except in accordance with Regulation III7.(b) or (c)).

TABLE I – TABLE OF PERMITTED INCREASES FOR
REVISED HANDICAPS

Handicaps plus to 34 may go up 2 strokes.
Handicap 35 may go up 1 stroke.

A handicap limited by the Table of Permitted Increases for Revised Handicaps shall be marked with an asterisk until the calculation of live scores results in a handicap equal to or less than that held.

(b) Minimum Number of Scores to be Returned

Handicap Categories E, D, C. To retain a handicap, a player with handicap 36★ – 10 must have returned at least four scores.

Handicap Category B. To retain a handicap, a player with handicap 9–4 must have returned at least six scores in Qualifying Competitions.

Exception: If a player with handicap 8 or 9 prior to Revision has returned at least four scores (not necessarily in Qualifying Competitions) the handicap shall not lapse, but shall be calculated in accordance with the Regulations governing handicaps 18–10 and Table I – the Table of Permitted Increases for Revised Handicaps.

Handicap Category A. To retain a handicap a player with handicap 3 or under must have returned at least ten scores in Qualifying Competitions. Only six of these may be from a Home Course, and the remaining four must be from at least two different Away Courses.

Exceptions: (a) If a player with handicap 2 or 3 prior to Revision has returned at least six scores in Qualifying Competitions, the handicap shall not lapse, but shall be calculated in accordance with Regulations governing handicaps 9–4 and the Table I – Table of Permitted Increases for Revised Handicaps.

(b) If a player with handicap 1 or under prior to Revision has returned ten scores in Qualifying Competitions, but not the necessary Away Scores, the handicap shall not lapse, but shall be increased by two strokes and marked with an @ until the necessary Away Scores have been returned.

(c) Lapsed Handicaps

A handicap lapses if a player has not returned the minimum number and types of scores necessary to retain a handicap (see (b) above). When a player's handicap has lapsed she does not have a valid handicap until the conditions have been fulfilled to regain it (see (d) below) and is ineligible to enter competitions.

(d) To Regain a Handicap which has Lapsed

Handicap Categories E, D, C. To regain a handicap which has lapsed, a player whose most recent handicap was in Category E, D or C, (36*–10) must return the number of Extra Day Scores necessary to increase the number of 'live' scores to four. The handicap shall then be calculated in accordance with Regulations, but it shall be limited by Table II – Table of Permitted Increases for Lapsed Handicaps set out below and must be confirmed, before use, by the player's Handicap Secretary.

TABLE II – TABLE OF PERMITTED INCREASES FOR LAPSED HANDICAPS

(i) If lapsed for less than one year the handicap shall be limited to two strokes higher than that last held.

(ii) For each year in excess of one the handicap may be increased by a further stroke. (The part year in which the handicap is regained counts as a whole year.)

EXAMPLES:

Handicap Lapsed on	Handicap regained during	Period Handicap lapsed	Max Inc over prev H'cap
(i) 31 January 1989	1993-1994(LGU year)	5 years	6 strokes
(ii) " " 1990	"	4 years	5 strokes
(iii) " " 1991	"	3 years	4 strokes
(iv) " " 1992	"	2 years	3 strokes
(v) " " 1993	"	less than 1 year	2 strokes

A handicap limited by the Table of Permitted Increases for Lapsed Handicaps shall be marked with an asterisk.

Handicap Category B. To regain a handicap which has lapsed, a player whose most recent handicap was in Category B (9–4) must return the necessary Extra Day Scores which together with the 'live' Qualifying Competition Scores make a total of six, except that a player with fewer than two 'live' Qualifying Competition Scores is only required to return four Extra Day Scores. The handicap shall be increased in accordance with Table II – Table of Permitted Increases for Lapsed

Handicaps, by the maximum permitted increase and must be confirmed, before use, by the player's Handicap Secretary. If the regained handicap is in Category B the handicap shall be marked with an @ until scores returned fulfil all the conditions necessary for this category of player.

Handicap Category A. To regain a handicap which has lapsed, a player whose most recent handicap was in Category A (3 and under) must return the necessary Extra Day Scores which together with the 'live' Qualifying Competition Scores make a total of ten, except that a player with fewer than six 'live' Qualifying Competition Scores is only required to return four Extra Day Scores. The handicap shall be increased in accordance with Table II – Table of Permitted Increases for Lapsed Handicaps by the maximum permitted increase and must be confirmed, before use, by the player's Handicap Secretary. If the regained handicap is in Category A or B the handicap shall be marked with an @ until scores returned fulfil all the conditions necessary for the player's category.

Note: Any Extra Day Scores used to regain a lapsed handicap, Category A or B, may only be used.

Transition to a Higher Category. The number of Extra Day Scores required to regain a handicap by a player in Category A or B shall be determined after taking into account the 'live' Qualifying Competition Scores and Table II – Table of Permitted Increases for Lapsed Handicaps. Players are only required to return a maximum of four Extra Day Scores before regaining a handicap. If the regained handicap is in Category A or B it shall be marked with an @ until scores returned fulfil all the conditions necessary for the player's category. When the appropriate scores have been returned, the handicap shall be calculated in accordance with Regulations and shall be marked with an asterisk until the calculation results in a handicap equal to or less than the regained handicap.

Note: A player whose most recent handicap was in Category A or B and permitted by Table II: Table of Permitted Increases for Lapsed Handicaps to be increased to Category C, D or E, is required to return the necessary Extra Day Scores to increase the number of 'live' scores to four.

7. Special Categories of Handicap

(a) **Juniors.** An LGU Junior handicap (limit 45) may be obtained and held by any girl who is a junior, ie who has not reached her twelfth birthday on 1 January, by returning two scores over nine specified holes. Any nine holes on the course may be chosen to make up the round, at the discretion of the club, and a special SS for those holes must be obtained from the National Organisation. Each score returned, and the special SS for the nine holes, shall be doubled in order to arrive at the number of strokes above SS Handicaps will be reduced in accordance with Regulations (one card 45–30, etc). Juniors may hold a standard LGU handicap but may not hold both.

To retain a Junior LGU handicap two strokes over nine holes must be returned annually. An LGU Junior handicap shall be acceptable for all junior competitions, and these Regulations shall apply to all players with Junior handicaps. Handicap Certificates for LGU Junior handicaps will be issued by the Handicap Secretary and *the date and year when the player will attain her twelfth birthday must be entered on the Handicap Certificate.*

(b) **Former Professional Golfers.** On reinstatement as an amateur a player who has been a professional golfer must apply for a handicap to the Administrator, LGU. The Executive Council shall, at their discretion, allot a handicap of not more than Scratch on the basis of live scores returned during the player's period of probation in accordance with the Regulations governing handicaps of 3 and under. For the first two years after reinstatement the player's Handicap Secretary must submit all scores returned twice yearly on 1 January and 1 July to the Administrator, LGU, The Scores, St. Andrews, Fife, KY16 9AT. Handicaps will be reviewed by the Executive Council and revised at their discretion.

(c) **After Serious Illness and Disablement.** A person wishing to regain a handicap or have her handicap reassessed after serious illness or disablement may apply through her Club Committee to the National Organisation with all relevant details, including a minimum of four live scores returned, so that consideration may be given to the circumstances and the player may obtain a realistic handicap.

Handicaps shall be adjusted in accordance with Regulations.

(d) **Individual Members and Visitors from Overseas.** The handicaps of Individual Members of the LGU or of the National Organisations shall be managed by the Administrator of the LGU or the Secretary of the appropriate National Organisation. All scores returned must be countersigned by the Handicap Secretary of the club at which they were returned and forwarded to the appropriate Secretary, who will act as Handicap Secretary for these players.

Handicaps of visitors from overseas who are not annual playing members of an affiliated club in Great Britain or Ireland shall be managed by the Administrator of the LGU, to whom scores should be forwarded after countersignature as above.

(e) **Senior Veterans and Disabled Players.** Where a club has members who do not normally play 18 holes but who wish to play competitive golf informally, it is suggested that special handicaps be allotted by the Committee on the basis of nine-hole scores doubled. The Committee should specify which nine holes are to be played and allot for those holes a 'scratch score', which should also be doubled to arrive at the handicap. *Handicaps so obtained are not LGU handicaps and are not valid for any purpose for which an LGU handicap is required.*

8. Membership of More than One Club

(a) A member belonging to more than one affiliated club must inform the Ladies' Secretary and Handicap Secretary of each club of the other affiliated clubs to which she belongs and also of any scores (together with Scratch Score) which may affect her handicap.

(b) Handicap Secretary. If a player is a member of more than one club she must decide which club she wishes to be her Home Club for handicap purposes and notify the Ladies' Secretary of that club accordingly. A player's Handicap Secretary shall be the Handicap Secretary of her Home Club.

(c) A member changing her Home Club must ask for a copy of her Handicap Register Form and take it with her Handicap Certificate to the Handicap Secretary of her new Home Club.

(d) A member joining an additional club must inform the Ladies' Secretary and the Handicap Secretary of such club of her existing or lapsed handicap, and of the scores, with relative dates, on which it was gained, and also the names of all clubs of which she is or has been a member.

(e) An annual playing member of a club affiliated to the LGU, who also has membership of a club under the jurisdiction of a different handicapping system, must return all scores which might affect her LGU handicap to her LGU Handicap Secretary, or in accordance with the Note to Regulation III4.(b) in the case of scores from non-LGU-affiliated courses overseas. Her handicap at her non-LGU-affiliated club, is NOT an LGU handicap and may be different from her LGU handicap. The use of her LGU handicap is mandatory only in competitions run by an organisation affiliated to the LGU. It is up to the competition committee of the host club to state which handicap must be used in a competition run under the jurisdiction of a different Handicapping System.

For details of the following, please refer to the Lady Golfer's Handbook:

- Responsibilities of Affiliated Clubs and of the National Organisations in relation to Handicapping, Competitions and Other Matters
- Scratch Scores
- LGU Tees and Teeing Grounds in Play
- Starting Places
- Handicap Records and Certificates
- LGU Silver and Bronze Medal Competitions
- LGU Gold and Silver Medal Competitions
- LGU Challenge Bowl Competitions
- Coronation Foursomes Competition
- LGU Pendant Competition
- Australian Spoons Competitions

UNITED STATES GOLF ASSOCIATION HANDICAP SYSTEM

INTRODUCTION

The United States Golf Association's handicap system is extremely detailed and incorporates features which make it a more accurate measure of a player's ability than any other handicapping method. It is also extremely comprehensive, filling a volume of 98 pages. What follows is therefore a potted version outlining how the system works. Readers wanting the complete system can order the booklet, USGA Handicapping System, by phoning 1-800-336-446 or by writing to the USGA Order Department, United States Golf Association, PO Box 708, Far Hills, New Jersey 07931-2300, USA.

USGA HANDICAP FORMULA

1. USGA Handicap Index Formula

A USGA Handicap Index is determined by a golf club or authorised golf association as follows:

a. Determine the handicap differentials by subtracting the corresponding USGA Course Rating from each of the last 20 adjusted gross scores and multiplying each resulting value by 113. Divide this result in each case by the corresponding USGA Slope Rating and round off to the nearest tenth.

b. Total the lowest 10 handicap differentials and multiply the result by .096. Delete all numbers after the tenths digit. (Do not round off to the nearest tenth.)

c. Effective 1992, apply Section 5-2 for golfers with two or more eligible tournament scores.

Handicap Differentials
A handicap differential is computed by determining the difference between the adjusted gross score and the USGA Course Rating, multiplying the difference by 113, dividing the resulting figure by the USGA Slope Rating and rounding off to the nearest tenth.

a. Plus Differential
When the adjusted gross score is *higher* than the Course

Rating, the handicap differential is a *plus* figure. Following is an example for a course with a USGA Course Rating of 71.5 and a USGA Slope Rating of 125:

Adjusted gross score	95
USGA Course Rating	71.5
Difference	23.5
Handicap differential	$\dfrac{113 \times (23.5)}{125} = 21.3$

b. Minus Differential

When the adjusted gross score is *lower* than the Course Rating, the handicap differential is a *minus* figure. Following is an example for a course with a USGA Course Rating of 71.5 and a USGA Slope Rating of 125:

Adjusted gross score	69
USGA Course Rating	71.5
Difference	−2.5
Handicap differential	$\dfrac{113 \times (-2.5)}{125} = -2.3$

2. Reduction Of Handicap Index For Exceptional Tournament Performance (Note: Implemented 1992)

Definitions

Tournament Score – A 'tournament score' is a score made in formal competition supervised by a golf club, golf association or other agency. Prizes are generally awarded. A 'T' shall be inserted beside a tournament score when it is posted for handicap purposes to distinguish it from other scores. (Examples: scores made in any championship, inter-club and intra-club competitions, member-guest tournaments, invitationals and pro-ams.)

Eligible Tournament Score – An 'eligible tournament score' is a tournament score contained within the player's last twenty scores or any scores made within the current year.

a. Purpose

The following procedure is to be used for the reduction of a Handicap Index when a player consistently scores much better in competitions than in informal games. To be used, the procedure requires that a player have two or more eligible tournament scores and a minimum of two tournament score differentials which are at least three strokes better than the player's current Handicap Index.

b. Determination of USGA Handicap Index Reduction
Apply the following procedures to determine the reduction in USGA Handicap Index, if any:

(1) Calculate the tournament score differentials by subtracting the USGA Course Rating from each eligible tournament score; multiply the result by 113 and divide by the USGA Slope Rating for each course played. Example: A player with a USGA Handicap Index of 17.6 who has three eligible tournament scores in his record; his lowest two are an 82 and 83, scored on a course with USGA Course Rating of 70.6 and a Slope Rating of 130.

	Lowest T-Score	2nd Lowest T-Score
Tournament score	82	83
Less USGA Course Rating	−70.6	−70.6
	11.4	12.4
Times 113 divided by Slope Rating of course played	$\frac{11.4 \times 113}{130} = 9.9$	$\frac{12.4 \times 113}{130} = 10.8$
Tournament Score Differential	9.9	10.8

(2) Select the two lowest tournament score differentials. Subtract the second lowest of these differentials from the player's current Handicap Index. If the result is 3.0 or greater, continue.

Example:
Handicap Index	17.6
Less Second Lowest Differential	−10.8
	6.8

This number is greater than 3.0, continue.

(3) Average the two lowest tournament score differentials by adding them together and dividing the sum by 2.

Example:

$$9.9 \atop +10.8 \over 20.7 \qquad \frac{20.7}{2} \qquad = 10.35$$

Add to this result the Exceptional Tournament Performance Limit in the following table corresponding to the total number of eligible tournament scores. This result is the reduced USGA Handicap Index for exceptional tournament performance. The result must be at least 1.0 less than the original Handicap Index, otherwise no adjustment is made.

Total number of eligible tournament scores	Exceptional tournament performance limit
2	3.0
3	3.5
4	4.0
5	4.3
6 or more	4.5

Example:

Average of Two Lowest Tournament Score Differentials	10.35
Select Number from Table Above Corresponding to Three Eligible Tournament Scores	+3.5
Sum	13.85
Round Off for Reduced Handicap Index	13.9

Since this reduced Handicap Index (13.9) is at least 1.0 less than the original Handicap Index (17.6), 13.9 becomes the player's new USGA Handicap Index.

c. Reporting Requirements

Golf associations and computational service companies shall report any Handicap Index reduction under this procedure to the golf club and, if computational reports are provided to the golf association, the service company shall also report any Handicap Index reductions to the golf association.

d. Handicap Committee Review of Reduction

A golf club Handicap Committee shall review all Handicap Index reductions made under this procedure. The Handicap Committee can override reductions if warranted for a specific reason.

3. Fewer than 20 scores available

a. Fewer than 5 Scores: no Handicap

A USGA Handicap Index shall not be issued to a player who has returned fewer than five acceptable scores.

b. 5 to 19 Scores

When at least 5 but fewer than 20 acceptable scores are available, the formula used to determine a USGA Handicap Index is as follows:

(1) Determine the number of handicap differentials to be used from the following table:

Column I *Differentials available*	Column II *Differentials to be used*
5 or 6	Lowest 1
7 or 8	Lowest 2
9 or 10	Lowest 3
11 or 12	Lowest 4
13 or 14	Lowest 5
15 or 16	Lowest 6
17	Lowest 7
18	Lowest 8
19	Lowest 9

(2) Determine handicap differentials in accordance with the procedure in Section 4.

(3) Average the lowest handicap differentials to be used from column II.

(4) Multiply this result by .96.

(5) Delete all numbers after the tenths digit (do not round off to the nearest tenth).

(6) Effective 1992, apply Section 5-2 for golfers with two or more eligible tournament scores.

Example: 11 scores available (Column I)

Total of lowest 4 differentials (Column II)	103.5
Average (103.5 divided by 4)	25.875
Multiply average by .96	24.84
Delete all numbers after the tenths digit	24.8
USGA Handicap Index is	24.8

(Note: Assuming Section 5-2 does not apply)

4. Course Handicap

A player does not play off his USGA Handicap Index. Rather, he converts the USGA Handicap Index to a Course Handicap and plays off the Course Handicap.

(Exception: A player with a USGA Handicap Index who plays at a course without a Slope Rating shall play off his Home Course Handicap.)

A Course Handicap is determined by multiplying the USGA Handicap Index by the USGA Slope Rating and dividing by 113. The resulting figure is rounded off to the nearest whole number (.5 is rounded upward).

5. Home Course Handicap

A 'Home Course Handicap' is a player's Course Handicap from the tees most frequently used by the membership as established by the club. Optionally, Home Course Handicaps may be printed on handicap records and cards.

Course Handicap Tables based on appropriate Slope Ratings for conversion of USGA Handicap Indexes to Course Handicaps are issued to golf clubs by authorised golf associations. These Tables should be displayed on or near the first tee and posted in the clubhouse.

USGA COURSE RATING: DEFINITIONS, PROCEDURE

1. Definitions

a. Scratch Golfer

(1) Man – The scratch golfer is an amateur player who plays to the standard of the stroke-play qualifiers competing at the U.S. Amateur Championship. A male scratch golfer can hit tee shots an average of 250 yards and can reach a 470 yard hole in two shots.

(2) Woman – The scratch golfer is an amateur player who plays to the standard of the match-play qualifiers competing at the U.S. Women's Amateur Championship. A female scratch golfer can hit tee shots an average of 210 yards and can reach a 400 yard hole in two shots.

b. Effective Playing Length

'Effective playing length' is the measured length of the golf course plus any adjustments to that length for factors such as unusual roll, elevation changes, forced lay-ups and dog-legs, prevailing wind and altitude above sea level which make the course play longer or shorter than its measured length.

c. Yardage Rating

'Yardage rating' is the evaluation of the playing difficulty of a course based on yardage only *(Definition 19a)*.

d. Obstacle Factors

'Obstacle factors' are hazards, natural features, vegetation and playing conditions found on the golf course which make it play harder or easier than an average course with the same effective playing length.

e. USGA Course Rating

'USGA Course Rating' is the evaluation of the playing difficulty of a course for scratch players under normal course and weather conditions *(Definition 19b)*. Course Rating is expressed in strokes and decimal fractions of a stroke, and is based on yardage and other obstacles to the extent that they affect the scoring ability of a scratch player.

Courses are rated by authorised golf associations, not by individual clubs. *(See Section 19.)*

Note: Yardage Rating and Course Rating are not to be confused with par, which for handicapping is too coarse a gauge of playing difficulty; par for two courses differing 440 yards in length might be identical, but the Yardage Rating of the longer course would be two strokes higher than the rating of the shorter course.

f. Bogey Golfer

A 'bogey golfer' is one with a USGA Handicap Index of 17.5 to 22.4 for men and 21.5 to 26.4 for women. A male bogey golfer can hit tee shots an average of 200 yards and can reach a 370 yard hole in two shots. A female bogey golfer can hit tee shots of 150 yards and can reach a 280 yard hole in two shots.

g. Bogey Rating

A 'bogey rating' is determined by evaluating the effective playing length and obstacle factors from the standpoint of the bogey golfer. It is equivalent to the average of the better-half of a bogey golfer's scores under normal playing conditions.

h. USGA Slope Rating

'Slope Rating' is the USGA's measure of the relative playing difficulty of a course for players with handicaps above scratch, whereas Course Rating is based solely on difficulty for the scratch player. The lowest Slope Rating is 55 and the highest is 155. The standard Slope Rating for men and women is 113.

2. CONDITIONS FOR RATING

a. Placement of Tee-markers and Holes

On the day a course is to be rated, the club should:

(1) Place tee-markers opposite the permanent yardage markers from which measurements will be made. *(See Section 16.)*

(2) Cut the hole in each green at an average location commonly used during maximum play. This should be a fairly easy location, probably near the centre of the green.

There is a tendency to set up the course to play long and hard. This will result in a higher rating which will reduce handicaps for club members.

b. Normal Playing Conditions

Courses should be rated under conditions normal for seasons of maximum play.

c. Rules of Golf

Course Rating shall be predicated on observance of the Rules of Golf. Any local rules must conform with the spirit of the Rules of Golf and USGA policy. *(See Section 12.)*

3. PROCEDURES FOR RATING COURSES

a. Procedure

Step 1 – Effective playing length is obtained from official

measurements of the course and an evaluation of the factors which cause the course to play significantly longer or shorter than its measured length *(Section 18-3b)*. Yardage *must be measured accurately*. An error of only 22 yards in the overall length will change the rating by 0.1 stroke for men. An error of only 18 yards will change the rating by 0.1 stroke for women.

Step 2 – Yardage Ratings for both scratch and bogey golfers are determined by applying the effective playing length to the USGA Yardage Rating formulae *(Section 18-4)*.

Step 3 – Course Rating is the scratch Yardage Rating of a course modified by the obstacle factors as they affect the scratch player.

Step 4 – Bogey Rating is the bogey Yardage Rating of a course modified by the obstacle factors as they affect the bogey player.

Step 5 – Slope Rating is the difference between the Bogey Rating and the Course Rating multiplied by 5.381 for men and by 4.24 for women.

b. Effective Playing Length

On each hole, the Rating Team evaluates the following factors. Their effect is converted to yardage which is added to, or subtracted from, the measured length to yield effective playing length. Effective playing length, in turn, is applied to the Yardage Rating formulae to produce scratch and bogey Yardage Ratings

(1) Roll
Unirrigated and thin fairways and downhill landing areas result in the ball rolling farther than the normal 25 yards. Irrigated and lush fairways and uphill landing areas result in the ball rolling less than 25 yards.

(2) Elevation
Holes which are uphill from tee to green play longer than those which are downhill from tee to green.

(3) Dog-leg
Holes in the fairway bends short of the normal drive zone will force the player to hit less than a full tee-shot.

(4) Prevailing Wind
Even though there may be as many holes with the wind

as against, a constant wind, as on a seaside course, makes play more difficult.

(5) Altitude Above Sea Level

The ball will carry a greater distance in high altitudes. The Yardage Rating of a course at an altitude of 2,000 feet or higher is adjusted downward to compensate.

c. Obstacle Factors

On each hole the Rating Team evaluates ten obstacle factors on a scale of 0 to 10 considering separately their effect on scratch and bogey players. When the rating process has been completed, units for each factor are totalled and multiplied by a relative weight factor. The resulting factors are then totalled and applied to scratch and bogey formulas which convert the weighted ratings to strokes. These Obstacle Stroke Values, which may be positive or negative, are added to the Yardage Ratings to produce the USGA Course Rating and Bogey Course Rating. The following obstacles are rated:

(1) Topography

Difficulty of stance in the landing area and the vertical angle of shot from the landing area into the green.

(2) Fairway

The effective width and depth of the landing area, which can be reduced by a dog-leg, trees or fairway slope.

(3) Recoverability and Rough

The existence of rough and other penalising factors in the proximity of the landing area and around the green.

(4) Out of Bounds/Extreme Rough

The existence of out of bounds in the proximity of the landing area and around the green; extreme rough which is similar in effect to out of bounds.

(5) Water Hazards

The existence of water hazards in the proximity of the landing area and around the green.

(6) Trees

The strategic location, size, height and number of trees.

(7) Bunkers

The existence of bunkers in the proximity of the landing area and around the green.

(8) Green Target

The size, firmness, shape and slope of a green in relation to the normal length of the approach shot.

(9) Green Surface

The contour and normal speed of the putting surface.

(10) Psychological

The mental effect on play created by the proximity of obstacles to a target area.

4. YARDAGE RATING FORMULAE

Yardage ratings are obtained by using the following formula:

a. Scratch Yardage Rating for Men

$$\text{Scratch Yardage Rating} = \frac{\text{Effective Playing Length of Course}}{220} + 40.9$$

Example: If the effective playing length of the course is 6,419 yards, Scratch Yardage Rating for men is calculated as follows:

$$\text{Scratch Yardage Rating} = \frac{6,419}{220} + 40.9 = 29.18 + 40.9$$

Scratch Yardage Rating = 29.2 + 40.9 = 70.1

Glossary

Address A golfer has addressed his ball as soon as he has taken his stance and grounded his club behind the ball. In a hazard, where it is not permitted to ground the club, taking a stance constitutes the address. The importance of the definitions is that if a ball moves after a player has addressed it, he is judged to have caused the ball to move and must count a penalty stroke.

Advice Any suggestion which could influence a golfer in making up his mind how to play, what club to use or the method of playing a stroke is advice. It can be sought or accepted only from a player's partner or either of their caddies. Information on general or local rules is not advice, nor is information about the line of play for a hole.

Albatross A score of three below par for a hole.

Alignment relationship between the player's body and the target line.

Arc Swing path of the club head.

Attending the flag A player is entitled to have the flag attended and held up to indicate the position of the hole at any time. On the green it is an infringement for a ball (played from on the green) to strike an unattended flagstick.

Back marker The player with the lowest handicap in a match. It is customary to compute strike allowances for matches by reducing the back marker's handicap to scratch.

Baffie Type of obsolete wooden club approximating to the modern 4 wood.

Best ball A match in which one player competes against the best ball of two or three other players.

Birdie A score of one below the par for a hole.

Bisque A handicap stroke which a player can elect to take at any time

during a match.

Blade To strike the ball with the leading edge, thus topping the shot. Sometimes played deliberately.

Blaster A broad-soled wedge.

Block Failure to clear the hips, thus bringing the club head into the ball in an open position and sending the ball out to the right of the fairway.

Bogey Standard American terminology (and spreading) for a score of one more than the par for a hole. Thus double-bogey, triple-bogey etc. Derives from the obsolescent system of rating golf courses according to the number of strokes a scratch player would be expected to take, therefore on longer and more difficult holes a stroke higher than par.

Brassie Old term for 2 wood.

Bulger Driver with a pronouncedly convex face.

Bunker Hazard consisting of an area of bare earth, or sand, usually in the form of a depression. Grass banks and artificial walls of bunkers are not part of the hazard.

Bye A secondary match played over the remaining holes after the main match has been completed.

Caddie A person employed to carry a player's clubs and offer advice. Players are responsible for the actions of their caddies and suffer penalties for any infringement of rule by their caddies.

Casual water Any temporary accumulation of water which is clearly visible after the player has taken his stance. Snow and ice may be treated as casual water or loose impediments at the discretion of

Chip A low, running shot played from just off the green.

Close To address the ball with the toe of the club advanced, or in the shut position.

Come off the shot To raise the

body before impact, thus causing the club head to strike high on the ball, thus causing a 'thin'.

Competitor Player in a stroke-play competition. A fellow competitor is a player he accompanies during play and may be his marker. A fellow competitor is not a partner within the rules.

Cut General term to denote a shot, deliberate or accidental, which causes the ball to move from left to right through the air. It thus covers both fades and slices.

Dead A ball is said to be dead when it lies so close to the hole as to make the putt a formality.

Dip Ducking movement on the downswing.

Divot A slice of turf displaced in making a shot. It is one of the canons of golf etiquette that divots should be replaced and firmly trodden into position.

Dormie, Dormy A player (or side) is said to be dormie when he is as many holes up in the match as there are holes left to be played and he therefore cannot be beaten. The expression is believed to derive from the French verb dormir since the player can go to sleep and still not be beaten.

Draw An intentional stroke which causes the ball to move in a controlled manner from right to left through the air.

Duck hook A shot which causes the ball to come off the club-head low and curving violently to the left.

Eagle A score of two under the par for a hole.

Eclectic A total arrived at by taking the best scores at each hole from a number of stroke-play cards returned by the same player.

Equipment Anything used, worn or carried by a player or his caddie, including golf carts and trolleys, but not his ball in play.

Explosion Sand shot in which the club face enters the sand behind the ball.

Extension Stretching of the arms on the follow through.

Fade An intentional stroke which causes the ball to move from left to right through the air in a controlled manner.

Fairway The mown portion of the playing area of a course between the tee and green. The rules of golf do not distinguish between fairways and rough (although special local rules may). In the rules, all of a course except the teeing ground and the green of the hole being played, and all hazards on the course, are defined as 'through the green'.

Fat A golfer is said to have hit the ball 'fat' when his club-head contacts the ground before striking the ball. Also used to describe the heart of the green – for example: 'I ignored the Rag and aimed for the fat of the green'.

Featherie Early type of golf ball traditionally made by stuffing a top-hatful of feathers into a hide casing.

Flagstick Movable indicator to mark the position of a hole. Colloquially referred to as pin, flag or stick.

Flyer, Flying lie A lie where grass or other vegetation intervenes between club-face and ball at impact, causing the shot to go further than normal.

Fore! Conventional golfer's cry to warn players ahead of an approaching ball.

Forecaddie A person employed by a competition committee to mark the landing of golf balls, especially on blind holes and in areas of excessive rough.

Forward press Slight forward movement of the hands at the address, designed to eliminate muscular tension.

Four-ball A match in which two players play their better ball against the better ball of two other partners.

Foursome A form of partner golf in which players take alternate shots at the same ball. Commonly known as Scotch Foursomes in America.

Grain (nap) Direction of oblique

growth of grass on a green.

Green The prepared putting surface. A ball is on the green when any part of it touches the green.

Greensome A modification of foursomes golf, with both partners driving at each hole and selecting the preferred ball with which to complete the hole in alternate strokes.

Ground under repair Any part of the course marked as such by the committee and material piled for removal.

Guttie Obsolete type of ball made from gutta percha.

Half A hole completed in the same net scores by both sides in matchplay is said to result in a half, or to be halved. Also used in the same sense to describe the result of a drawn match.

Hanging lie A lie on sloping ground which forces the golfer to play from an uneven stance.

Hazard Any bunker or water hazard defined as such by the committee.

Heavy Making contact with clubface too low, thus causing the club to dig into the ground and reduce the power of the shot.

Heel Innermost part of the club sole. Also a shot struck from inward area of wooden club-face.

Hole The hole is standardised at 4in in diameter (108mm) and at least 4in (100mm) deep. If a liner is used it must be sunk at least 1in below the surface.

Holed A ball is judged to be holed when all of it lies with the circumference of the hole and below the lip. Honour The privilege of playing first from the tee.

Hooding Tilting club-face at address to reduce the angle of loft while keeping the face square to the target line.

Hook An unintentional stroke which causes the ball to fly from right to left through the air in an uncontrolled manner.

Hosel The neck of an iron club into which the shaft is fitted.

Jigger A specialist club for run-up shots.

Lag A putt which is deliberately run up to the hole with the prime intention of leaving an easy tap-in putt to follow.

Like A player is said to be 'playing the like' when he is taking a shot which makes his score the same as his opponent's.

Line of play Usually abbreviated to 'the line', as in 'What is the line on this hole?' Means the preferred route.

Links A golf course built on linksland by the sea. Sometimes used loosely as another term for a golf course of any kind.

Lob High shot played with lofted club designed to land softly with little backspin.

Local rules Rules formulated by local committees to cover special conditions on the course.

Loft The angle a club-face is set back from the perpendicular.

Loose impediments Natural objects, not fixed or growing. Includes stones if not firmly embedded, fallen twigs and leaves, dung, worms and insects, and casts made by them. Sand and loose soil are classified as loose impediments on the green but not through the green. Snow and ice may be classified as loose impediments or casual water, at the discretion of the player.

Lost ball A ball is declared to be lost if it is not found within five minutes; or if the owner puts another ball into play; or if the player formally abandons his ball, whether or not he searches for it; or if he plays any stroke with a provisional ball beyond the place where the original ball was likely to be.

Marker A person, often a fellow competitor, charged with keeping a competitor's score. It is, however, the responsibility of the player to ensure the accuracy of his score.

Mashie An old, lofted iron club roughly equivalent to a 5 iron.

Mashie-niblick An old club, as above, approximating to a 7 iron.

Match-play The form of golf which is contested on the number of holes won, rather than by the total number of strokes taken for a round (stroke-play). Special rules operate for match-play golf.

Medal play Stroke-play.

Moved ball A ball is judged to have moved if it comes to rest in another position. Rocking, or oscillation, does not count as movement for purposes of penalty at the address provided the ball settles back into its original position.

Mulligan The practice, quite unofficial, of allowing a player a 'free' second drive when his first shot is unsatisfactory.

Nap Sometimes called grain. It is the texture of a putting surface caused by grasses tending to lie in the same direction.

Nassau A form of wager involving a three-way bet: on the first nine holes, on the second nine, and a similar amount on the match as a whole.

Niblick An old club roughly equal to a 9 iron.

Observer A person appointed by the committee to help a referee decide questions of fact and report any infringements.

Obstruction Anything artificial erected, placed or left on the course, except boundary fences, walls and stakes and artificial roads and paths. The committee may decree any such to be an integral part of the course in which case the rules for relief from obstructions do not apply.

Odd A player is said to be playing the odd when he is taking a shot which makes his score one more than his opponent's.

Open To address the ball with the toe of the club laid slightly back.

Out of bounds A ball is out of bounds when all of it lies over a line drawn between the nearest inside points of boundary stakes. If a line is used to define a boundary the line itself is out of bounds.

Outside agency Any agency not part of the match. In stroke-play outside agencies include referees, markers, fellow competitors and observers.

Par The norm for a hole. In most countries par is set exclusively on length. Holes up to 250 yards are par-3; 251–475 yards are par-4; 476 yards and over are par-5.

Partner A player on the same side.

Penalty A stroke, or strokes, to be added to the score under the rules. Penalty strokes do not affect the order of play in foursomes or greensomes.

Pin high A shot finishing level with the flagstick is said to be pin high, therefore a perfect length but not necessarily straight.

Pitch A high, floating shot. Normally used to describe such shots played to a green.

Pivot Turning of the body during the backswing.

Plane Angle of swing arc in relation to the ground.

Plumb bob Method of holding up the putter between finger and thumb to determine which way a putt will break.

Press The act of spoiling a shot by hitting too hard. Also, in wagering, a subsidiary bet which can be instituted over the remaining holes when a side becomes two down in the main match.

Pull An unintentional shot which flies in a straight line to the left of the target.

Punch shot Stroke played with hands in front of the ball and wrists firm.

Push Opposite of pull. In this case the ball goes in a straight line to the right of the target.

Putt A stroke played with a putter.

Quit Deceleration of club head at impact.

Referee A person appointed by a committee to accompany players and rule on questions of fact and golf law. His decision is final.

Release Flexible action of the wrists as the club-head comes into the impact zone.

Round Robin A type of match-play competition in which every entrant plays against everyone else, the person with the most victories being the winner.

Rubber core A ball made by winding rubber thread under tension around a central core and then covering with a plastic casing. This is the universal method of manufacturing the highest grade balls.

Rub of the green The expression to cover the case of a moving ball being stopped or deflected by an outside agency. Commonly it is used to describe any piece of golfing luck, good or bad, for which there is no provision in the rules.

Sand-wedge Specialist club for playing recovery shots from sand.

Scratch The handicap mark of a first-class player. Methods of computing scratch ratings vary from country to country but loosely the term can be said to cover golfers who can regularly play par golf off the competition tees in summer conditions. Scratch players get no handicap allowance, hence scratch competitions are those in which no handicap strokes are given.

Shank (socket) A stroke in which the hosel, or neck, of the club makes contact with the ball, sending it off at an acute angle.

Skull To catch the ball a glancing blow with the sole of the club.

Sky To catch the ball with wooden club (usually) on upper rim of face, causing the ball to balloon.

Slice Unintentional shot which causes the ball to veer from left to right in an uncontrolled manner through the air.

Spoon Obsolescent term for 3 wood.

Stableford Form of golf in which players count one point for a score of one over the par for a hole, two points for par, three points for a birdie – and so on.

Stance The placing of the feet in position in preparation for making a stroke. A stance is not necessarily an address.

Stroke A forward movement of the club made with the intention of fairly striking the ball.

Stroke-play Also known as medal-play. The system of golf in which a player counts his total of strokes for a round.

Swing The entire action of playing a stroke.

Takeaway The start of the backswing.

Tee A peg for teeing the ball or the prepared area on which the teeing ground is sited.

Teeing ground A rectangular two club-lengths in depth measured back from a line between the markers.

Texas wedge American term for a shot played from off the green with a putter.

Thin Failure to keep the club-face low enough at impact to produce a Rush shot.

Three-ball A match in which three players each play against the two others.

Threesome A match in which one player plays against two partners playing alternate shots at one ball.

Through the green The whole area of the course except all hazards as well as the teeing ground and the green of the hole being played.

Top The action of striking the ball's top half, producing a low, scuttling shot.

Trap Colloquialism for bunker.

Waggle Preliminary movement of the club at address before making a stroke.

Wedge Broad-soled club designed for pitching.

Winter rules Special local rules employed by committees to protect the course in winter. Conventions vary from club to club and players should always check the local rules to determine the type and degree of relief which is permissible.

Index